# Social Analysis

# Social Analysis

*A Collaborative Method of Gaining Usable Scientific Knowledge of Social Institutions*

Ralph W. Rowbottom

 Heinemann · London

*Heinemann Educational Books Ltd*
London   Edinburgh   Melbourne   Auckland   Toronto
Hong Kong   Singapore   Kuala Lumpur   New Delhi
Nairobi   Johannesburg   Lusaka   Ibadan
Kingston


ISBN  0  435  82772  3  (*cased*)
       0  435  82773  1  (*limp*)
© Ralph Rowbottom 1977
First published 1977

H
61
R688

Published by Heinemann Educational Books Ltd
48 Charles Street, London W1X 8AH

Filmset in 'Monophoto' Baskerville 11 on 12 pt and
printed in Great Britain by
Richard Clay (The Chaucer Press), Ltd,
Bungay, Suffolk

# Preface

Many books and articles have been published on the Glacier Project which started in 1948 and the subsequent work which has developed from it in health, social welfare and certain other fields, centred on the Brunel Institute of Organization and Social Studies. All this work employs a particular approach or method which Elliott Jaques, who pioneered it, has described as 'social analysis'. In brief, this involves an active collaboration between those experiencing problems with the organization in which they find themselves and an outside consultant-cum-researcher, whose aim it is to help analyse the social nature of these problems, and the possibilities for change.

As a method of work it has proved potent, both in generating new organizational and social theories rich in implications, and in helping to achieve beneficial change.

The Glacier Project itself has provided a remarkable example of research and change which has continued in unbroken sequence for nearly thirty years, involving practically every aspect of the institutions, organization and procedures of a large modern manufacturing concern. The work at Brunel has been underway for nearly a decade. There are indications that it has had a significant effect on general organizational thinking and development throughout the National Health Service and in local authority Social Services Departments across the country – employers, all told, of something over a million people. A dozen or so major books (as well as many articles and papers) describing the results of all this have found readers throughout the world. Altogether the continuing work must by any reckoning be acknowledged as one of the largest sustained programmes of action research of our time, in this or any other country.

So far however, little has been written about the method itself. In 1964 Elliott Jaques produced a first paper on the subject relating it specifically to the Glacier Project.[1] In 1974 I myself and my co-authors attempted a further short statement in the context of the work on hospital organization.[2] Following two extended visits to the Brunel Institute of Organization and Social Studies, Professor William Westley of McGill University has written a paper which offers an outsider's assessment of the basic principles of social analysis and how social analysts actually work in practice.[3] These apart, information about the method has had to be disentangled as best as possible from various detailed accounts of substantive project-work.[4]

A previous text based on the Glacier Project carried the title 'Organization Analysis'. That however concerned itself solely with the substance of certain specific theories of organization resulting from the Glacier Project. By contrast 'social analysis', as we have said, refers to the method itself by which organizational problems may be explored in any context. (In retrospect it seems doubtful whether the conception of 'organization analysis', as standing for some specific brand of organizational theory, was a useful one. However 'social analysis' as an approach certainly possesses characteristics and unusual features of its own as will be shown, and thus justifies a distinctive label.)

Over the years a number of researchers to be counted in several dozens now have had the exciting and demanding experience of trying out this still-developing method. There has been continuous review and critical discussion of it. Much has been learnt from practice – both of what works and, needless to add, of what does not.

The time now appears ripe to attempt a more comprehensive statement. Reflection begins to reveal what appear to be important principles, not just relevant to subsequent research of the same type, but to greater questions of the general nature of social theory, social research and social change, and the relationship of the three.

It has become apparent for example, that the social-analytic method goes a long way in its own field to solving the perennial problem of how to get access to study social matters of real concern at first hand, and how to secure the commitment of those under study to produce information of genuine validity.

Again, it is evident that the method has served to bridge (or rather to avoid) those two terrible divides: of 'social theory' from 'social

[1] Jaques (1965c), 'Social Analysis and the Glacier Project'.
[2] Rowbottom et al. (1973), Hospital Organization, Appendix B.
[3] Westley (1975), 'Dialogue with Reality: A Study of Social Analysis'.
[4] The accumulated social-analytic literature is briefly reviewed in Appendix B to the main text.

practice' on the one hand, and of 'social theory' from 'empirical research' on the other. In social analysis, theory emerges naturally out of the study of empirical problems, and new ideas and conceptions are put to use and test in the process which just as naturally follows. Social analysis does not merely produce scientific knowledge that broadens the general outlook: it provides knowledge which is immediately *usable*.

Finally, it has become apparent that the approach has important things to say about the hoary old question of what being 'scientific' in social affairs really means. Practice has demonstrated for example that it is possible to reach objective, tested generalizations in certain social matters without leaning exclusively on the large-scale survey. It has also suggested that there is a new kind of scientific proposition to be recognized in social sciences. It is one that is based on an 'action' as opposed to a 'behavioural' view of man, and one which is fundamentally different from the strict deterministic or causal laws to be found in the natural sciences.

It seems therefore that a full-scale description and discussion of the social-analytic method may be of interest not only to those who might wish to try their own hand at it, but to social scientists in general. It also has things of relevance for all those who, though perhaps not strictly to be described as social scientists, work as it were at the borders of social science – management consultants, operational researchers, personnel and organizational specialists, community development workers and the like.

My own qualifications for attempting this major task are as follows. After a number of years in industry and commerce I joined the Glacier Metal Company as an internal consultant in 1963. There I became directly exposed to the social ideas and practices that had been developed, and were still developing, in that Company (although I did not at that time undertake any social-analytic work itself). In 1965 I moved to the Glacier Institute of Management which gave further opportunities to study these ideas and to try their validity in seminar discussions with people from a wide variety of other organizations and undertakings. After a further short spell in industry I came to Brunel in 1968 to work with Elliott Jaques and his colleagues. Since that time I have been involved full-time in social-analytic work in both the health and the social welfare fields (latterly, in the second case, as Director of the Social Services Organization Research Unit).

# Acknowledgements

In preparing the text I have been grateful for the comments and suggestions of many colleagues, particularly those of David Billis, Geoff Bromley, Alan Dale, Anthea Hey and Ken Knight. My profound debt to Elliott Jaques, the originator of many of the ideas and approaches to be discussed, will be obvious. He too has offered many specific comments which have helped to shape the actual text. I have sincere thanks to give to Stella Beckett for the many hours she has devoted to subjecting the final draft to the critical eye of the intelligent lay reader. Finally, I should like to record my thanks to Zena Pereira for her patient work in transmuting the most unpromising raw material into clear typescript.

# Contents

'The piecemeal engineer will, accordingly, adopt the method of searching for, and fighting against, the greatest and most urgent evils of society, rather than searching for, and fighting for, its greatest ultimate good. . . . the kind of experiment from which we can learn most is the alteration of one social institution at a time. For only in this way can we learn how to fit institutions into the framework of other institutions, and how to adjust them so that they work according to our intentions. And only in this way can we make mistakes, and learn from our mistakes, without risking repercussions of a gravity that must endanger the will to future reforms.'

Karl Popper
*The Open Society and Its Enemies*

'The positivist separation of knowledge and decision, of procedures for answering questions and procedures for solving problems, is itself premodern; it originated in a time when speechmakers could still celebrate the idyllic relationship of mind and power, when the ivory tower of the university could be contrasted with the hard reality of, say, government, when professors could be patronized by men of action. Today, questions and problems are so closely intermeshed that neither the theorist nor the practitioner can avoid reasoning about them in a single context and with equal intensity.'

Ralf Dahrendorf
*Essays in the Theory of Society*

PART I

# The Origins and General
# Nature of Social Analysis

# 1 Introduction

In social analysis three distinctive modern concerns are to be found in unusual combination.

The first is the idea of promoting radical changes in the way people function through the direct intervention of independent agents of professional stance – such typical modern figures as the psychotherapist, the social worker, the community worker or the specialist in organization development. These new 'change agents' (as they have been collectively described) are characterized by an approach significantly different from the more traditional ones of say the doctor, the charity worker, the expert adviser or the evangelist. Putting it broadly, their aim has been not to do things to people but to help them to do things for themselves. They have been occupied not just with treating people, succouring them, advising them or exhorting them, but with helping them to develop a better capacity to cope with their own problems or to enhance their own lives.

The rapid growth in those professionally employed in work of this kind is a phenomenon of the last hundred years or so. Its origin can be located perhaps in the pioneering attempts of Charcot, Janet and Freud to develop a 'talking cure' for mental disturbance. Psychoanalysis flourished, and its analytic approach and 'counselling ideology'[1] spread and took root in social work, probation work, marriage and child guidance, and many allied activities. During and immediately after the Second World War the approach began to be extended from work with individuals to work with small groups of those in distress or trouble, and thence to broader social organization. In the 1940s and 50s, at the Tavistock Institute of Human Relations in London and the National Training Laboratories in Bethel, Maine, psychoanalytic approaches were combined with Kurt

[1] Halmos (1965), *The Faith of the Counsellors*.

Lewin's ideas of 'real-life' experiment and change in social groups. Words like 'action research', 'social therapy' and 'sensitivity training'; 'planned change', 'change agent' and 'client system', were in the air. In the following years the emphasis shifted somewhat with an increasing use of systematic social survey. The conception of 'organization development' ('OD' as it is colloquially known) emerged, encompassing the activities of a growing band of social psychologists employed in problem-oriented work in large-scale organizations.[2] Historically, social analysis too stems from this broad growth, and, as we shall see, still shares many of the basic assumptions and beliefs which have nourished it.

The second element in social analysis, at any rate as it has now become, is a strong concern with social structure, or more exactly, with social institutions. It is again perhaps only in the last century, with the rapid development of anthropological and sociological study, that modern man has become so keenly aware of the influence of the particular culture he is born into, and of the particular social classes and groups to which he belongs, on his individual actions and beliefs. 'Human nature' is to some large extent, it seems, what society makes it. In each position or situation in which a person finds himself – as a parent or a child, a doctor or a patient, a foreman or a shop-steward – there already exist (for better or worse) established and searching requirements about how one ought to behave in such situations and about exactly what sort of role is to be played. Social analysis as it has developed has become increasingly concerned with this deeper, institutional structure.[3] Attention has shifted decisively away from more ephemeral matters, like the play of personality on personality, or the minute-by-minute dynamics of particular groups of people interacting face to face.

The concern of social analysis then is not just with helping people, but more specifically with helping them understand better the social institutions within which they interact, so that they may modify and improve them in a controlled way. This necessarily supposes that the people involved can act collectively to change their social structure.

[2] For general views of the development of this work with groups and organizations *see* Lippitt, Watson and Westley (1958), *The Dynamics of Planned Change*; Bradford, Gibb and Benne (1964), *Group Theory and Laboratory Method*; Bennis, Benne and Chin (1970), *The Planning of Change*; Bennis (1969), *Organization Development*; Foster (1972), *An Introduction to the Theory and Practice of Action Research in Work Organizations*. (Specific references to the Tavistock work are cited below.)

[3] The explicit study of social role is a comparatively recent undertaking in social science, dating from the 1930s. For a historical and comparative review of role-theory *see* Dahrendorf (1968a), 'Homo Sociologicus', and Banton (1965), *Roles*.

In other words, it necessarily supposes that the people concerned are organized in some way, or that they have some capacity to organize themselves.

The third main element in social analysis is the deep-rooted modern belief that a scientific approach to problems of all kinds, human as well as natural, offers in the long term greater prospects of mastery than even the best developed personal intuitions or most inspired trial-and-error technology. The adoption of a consciously scientific approach to social problems can again be dated within the last century. Significantly, its beginning was associated with the large-scale systematic survey, and it has tended to retain this same association since, a fact with which we shall have to come to terms later in the discussion.[4] As we shall see, the scientific element in social analysis does not, and cannot in principle, given its specific subject and approach, manifest itself through use of the large-scale survey, statistical analysis, control groups, and the like. Instead it manifests itself much more in concern with clarification of basic social concepts, the teasing out of linkages between them, and the evolution of testable institutional 'models' to guide collective action and interaction.

Social analysis then combines each of three elements. First and foremost, it is a problem-oriented activity, which involves continuous collaboration between those experiencing the problem and an external change agent, the 'social analyst'. Second, it is specifically concerned with problems of the social structure, the institutional framework, within which people interact in organized activity. And thirdly, it is concerned not just with the application, but with the generation, of true scientific knowledge about such matters.

As we have said, none of these three concerns is by itself unfamiliar in the modern world. However an activity which fuses all three does exhibit a certain novelty.

Thus, in the work of the various species of change agents referred to above, the emphasis has nearly always been on developing the maturity or capability of the individual or individuals concerned. Little or nothing has been done (aside from the social-analytic activities under consideration here) which could accurately be de-

---

[4] Charles Booth's comprehensive study of labour and life amongst the poor in London published in the last decade of the nineteenth century is often quoted as the main starting point of the flood of systematic, factual social surveys that followed, though earlier social surveys of various kinds had taken place. *See* Simey (1968), *Social Science and Social Purpose*, for an account of the origins of the empirical approach in sociology.

scribed as helping to develop better social institutions. Little or nothing has been done, for example, to clarify the roles expected of people in particular established positions, or the procedures which best mediate their discussions and disagreements. Little has been done to help reveal systematically the institutions needed in public or private undertakings in order to develop more effective kinds of products or services for the community, or to allow greater participation. in decision by those who actually provide them. Reasonable though this may be in work like counselling or psychotherapy, which is explicitly focused on the individual, it is strange perhaps that this should also be true, for example, of an activity which describes itself as 'organization development'.[5]

Then again, there has tended to be a sharp divide between the change agents and practitioners on the one hand, and the 'social scientists' on the other. The lack of sympathy between these two groups, if not their positive antagonism, has been notorious. For their part the change agents have tended to be more concerned with immediate practical results than developing or applying some body of scientifically validated knowledge or deep scientific theory. OD practitioners and other action researchers have claimed that the application of scientific knowledge is an essential element of their work.[6] But in reality the familiar yawning gap between social theory and practice seems to persist. A general perusal of the OD literature reveals few, if any, instances where fundamental concepts or propositions from social, psychological or political theory are actually put to work in helping to analyse the problems of clients. Although scientific methods are sometimes employed, as for example in the carrying out of systematic data collection or attitude surveys, the actual substance of analysis is nearly always formed in everyday, commonsense and unrefined terms. Where any systematic theorizing or conceptualization is attempted, it tends to be at a fairly primitive level and not to be readily relatable to the main established body of social and psychological science, such as it is.[7]

[5] Exceptions to this general statement may be noted in some degree in the later work at the Tavistock Institute, and associated developments at the Institute for Industrial Social Research in Trondheim, Norway, and the Work Research Institute in Oslo. See Rice (1963), *The Enterprise and Its Environment*; Miller and Rice (1967), *Systems of Organization*; Emery and Thorsrud (1969), *Form and Content in Industrial Democracy*; and Herbst (1974), *Socio-Technical Design*.

[6] *See*, for example, Beckhard (1969), *Organization Development*; Bennis, Benne and Chin (1970), *The Planning of Change*, p. 4.

[7] As, for example, in the conception of the 'managerial grid' described by Blake and Mouton (1969); or the conception of organizational 'differentiation' and

On the other hand the 'social scientists' – the psychologists, sociologists, economists and so on – have for the most part tended to avoid any direct intervention in the various more or less painful aspects of individual or social existence on which they have turned the beam of their academic scrutiny from time to time. This is not to say that they have refrained from critical comment on what they have revealed, or indeed on occasion from impassioned advocacy of general reform. (One thinks here, of the whole English school of social administration, starting with Booth and the Webbs in the late nineteenth century and including such names as Titmuss, Townsend and Abel-Smith in the twentieth.) But they have tended to avoid immediate involvement in the concrete instance with a view to actual amelioration or change.

In social analysis however these two latter strands – the practical concern in the immediate case, and the scientific interest in the general proposition – are welded firmly in the process of *collaborative exploration*. Here the analyst is able to make direct contact with, and to exert direct influence upon, immediate practical social issues. And by restricting himself severely to an elucidatory role, by striving for the utmost conceptual clarification of the problem in hand, by searching always for general linkages between the various social factors involved, he contrives to maintain intact his scientific status.

### 'Social Therapy' and The Glacier Project

Interestingly, the immediate origins of social analysis lie in work which, initially at any rate, was heavily slanted to a concern with matters of personal attitude rather than social structure. In 1948 a team of researchers from the Tavistock Institute under the leadership of Elliott Jaques started what was to develop into a very long and remarkable project at Glacier Metal (a medium-sized engineering company which manufactured metal bearings).

The Tavistock Institute of Human Relations had been founded two years earlier by a group of psychiatrists and social scientists concerned to bridge the gap between the various theoretical social sciences and practical problems of human relations in the family, industry and other parts of society. Its characteristic approach at that time has been variously described by its own members as the

---

'integration' by Lawrence and Lorsch (1969). Again, it might be argued that the Tavistock and associated work referred to in Note 5 provides some exceptions to this general statement.

'diagnosis and treatment of social problems', 'social doctoring', 'social therapy' and 'psychoanalytically-oriented, inter-disciplinary, social psychiatry'. However, in spite of the distinctive medical flavour, there was strong emphasis from the start on collaboration ('doing things *with* people') as opposed to technocracy ('doing things *to* people').[8]

The team at Glacier specifically did not wish to be seen as working solely with or for management, or solely with or for the workers, but with and on behalf of all members of the factory. The prior existence of a vigorous Works Council with representatives from all parts and levels of the factory allowed a means of satisfying this ambition. The jointly agreed conditions of work were as follows.[9]

(a) The Research Team is responsible to and reports to the Works Council.
(b) The Works Council has delegated a Project Sub-Committee which together with the Research Team will plan the programme and development of the Glacier Project.
(c) It is not the intention of the project that the Research Team should gather secret information from one person or group about another. The only material that will be of real value is information that is public and can be reported.
(d) Where any individual or group suggests a topic of study for the Research Team to look at, this shall only be done with the general approval of those likely to be affected by the results . . .

During the next three years a wide range of subjects was studied: problems of worker–management cooperation in the Works Council itself; relations amongst the workers' own representatives in the 'Works Committee'; and relations between various groups of managers at middle and top level.

During this first period much of the analysis was in terms of personal attitudes and personal interaction. The two following quotations from a subsequently published report of the work[10] may convey some of this flavour.

It was not just that the Managing Director was a person about whom his subordinates had such mixed and disturbing feelings: he was also a figure

---

[8] For general reviews of the Tavistock Institute of Human Relations, its origin and its subsequent development, *see* Brown, R. K. (1967), Trist (1967) and Rapoport (1970). *See also* a whole issue of the *Journal of Social Issues* edited by Elliott Jaques (1947) which was devoted to a collective statement of the Tavistock work and outlook at the time.
[9] Jaques (1951), *Changing Culture of a Factory*, pp. 13–14.
[10] *Changing Culture*, pp. 218, 219 and 93.

of authority, conjuring up all past experiences with authority, good and bad. It was because there was so much displacement on to the person of the Managing Director of private and distressing feelings that had to do not with him alone, that there was also worry and uncertainty in the group about tackling the problem of authority.

Referring to the increasing heat of the discussion, the consultant interpreted what again seemed to him to be an implicit statement of the workers' lack of confidence in their own management. He commented that the Shop Committee felt that a management 'who got talked out of their profits' were stooges to the rest of management in the company. In view of the rational explanations that had been given, he went on to say that many of these feelings represented attitudes towards past managements, which were being projected into the present situation.

The essence of the method, as it was seen at this time, was in helping groups to unearth and identify various resistances or concealed forces, which were preventing them from coming to grips with manifest problems which they faced – a process described as 'working through'. However, even at this time there were signs of the recognition of the importance of coming to grips with some of the substantive matters actually at issue, as well as with clearing away the psychological blocks to tackling them. For example, there was explicit discussion of the general nature of the executive authority of managers, and how it might receive continuing sanction through joint consultation and negotiation processes with workers and their representatives. There was discussion of the problems which arise when it is attempted to combine the role of a managing director in charge of a whole company operation with that of a general manager in a specific area at the next lower organizational level. There was discussion of the essential difference between the position of a delegate, who is bound by the specific instruction of his shop-floor constituents, and that of a representative who has freedom to act on his constituents' behalf as he judges best, within broad limits.

At the end of the initial three-year sponsored project Elliott Jaques was given a personal invitation to continue as a consultant in social matters, financed directly by the Company. As time went by, further published reports showed a decreasing concern with helping groups to become aware of and overcome their own unconscious resistances. Instead, attention was increasingly directed to the substantive problems under discussion: to such things as payment schemes and payment progression procedures; to the proper forms of procedure for avoiding disputes and for dealing with appeals; to questions of the precise structure of executive organization and of executive role relationships.[11] Moreover it was found to be useful to preface group discussions of these matters with confidential discussions with individual members, in which any attitudinal and psychological issues could be separated from structural matters and put in their proper perspective.

## Subsequent Work

By the early 1960s Jaques was able to look back over an uninterrupted period of some fifteen years' collaboration with Glacier Metal and take stock of the precise method of work which had eventually evolved, which he now explicitly referred to by the name 'social analysis'. His own succinct statement from this time bears repeating.[12]

> In essence . . . social-analysis requires an individual or individuals in an organization, with a problem concerning the working of the organization, who seek the help of an analyst in determining the nature of the problem. The analyst is independent in the sense that he is not personally embroiled in the organization and its problems; he is from outside. He offers analytical help; he does not urge a particular course of action. The individuals in the organization also remain independent: they decide what they are going to do, and do it. It is not for the social-analyst to arrogate to himself either the authority or the accountability of those with whom he is working.

By this time then, the concern was quite explicitly with analysing the nature of problems 'concerning the working of the organization'.

In 1961 a special establishment, the Glacier Institute of Management, was opened by the Company. Its prime aim was to provide a means of inducting their own managers in the various ideas and policies that had now accrued. However it also served to provide a point of ready access for the increasing number of outsiders who were now evincing interest in the project and its findings. Through the Institute contact was established with a wide circle of other concerns both in Britain and abroad, with other manufacturing and commercial firms, and with many nationalized industries and public services. Thus a forum was provided in which the generality and wider validity of the emerging products of social analysis

---

[11] *See* the subsequent Glacier Project literature described in Appendix B.

[12] Jaques (1965c), 'Social Analysis and the Glacier Project', p. 34.

could be tested and where necessary modified, through lecture, seminar and discussion.

In 1965 Elliott Jaques was appointed Professor in Social Institutions and Head of the School of Social Sciences at Brunel University. Under his supervision and with the sponsorship of central government, two new major social–analytic projects were launched, one in health services starting in 1967, and the other in local authority social services starting in 1969. (Both of these continue still at the time of writing.) Other more limited social-analytic projects have since been undertaken by Professor Jaques, the present author, and other colleagues at Brunel, including work with a government department, with a number of voluntary and professional associations and with the Church of England.[13]

In the Health Service Project a team of some eight or nine workers established contact with large numbers of hospital doctors, nurses, members of the paramedical professions (physiotherapists, occupational therapists, radiographers, pharmacists, laboratory technicians, etc.) administrators, engineers, builders and other hospital staff. The main concern in the early project activity was in exploring the nature of the working relationships, all more or less problematic, that arose between these various groups.[14] Study of these complex relationships involving as they did a rich mixture of specialized and professional skills on one hand, and the particular requirements inherent in therapeutic work on the other, revealed new patterns which it had not been possible to observe in the more straightforward industrial setting. This detailed exploration proved of great value in the next phase of the project, when members of the research team contributed to discussion about possible detailed organizational arrangements within a broad political framework already decided for the new integrated National Health Service that was to be introduced in 1974. At about this time the scope of the project was broadened to include the two other then-existing branches of health service – the family practitioners (doctors, dentists, etc.) and public health services. As the integrated health service came into being, discussions were undertaken at their invitation with

[13] At the time of writing a further major project under the direction of Professor Maurice Kogan, using a broadly social-analytic approach and directed to the functioning and organization of schools in the community, is underway. Professor Kogan acted also as the first Director of what started as the Hospital Organization Research Unit in the health services work described below.

[14] For published accounts of social-analytic work in the health field, see Appendix B.

a number of the newly appointed officers to see how their pre-designated roles and relationships worked out in practice, and what unexpected problems were arising. Important new topics of work were opened up in discussions with members of the governing bodies of the new statutory health authorities, and with members of the newly created 'community health councils' concerning such things as the meaning of community participation, and the nature of their individual and collective roles (some were also elected members of local authorities for example, and some were practising doctors or senior nurses). At about the same time a series of intensive projects were established in particular fields such as care of the mentally ill, care of the mentally handicapped, child guidance and geriatric services.

Throughout the whole activity a continuing series of conferences varying in length from one day to two weeks were organized at Brunel, and attended by many hundreds of professional practitioners, senior health service officers, and appointed members of statutory health authorities and community health councils. These conferences allowed the continued testing out in discussion of the generalizations of particular project findings, and at the same time a start to the job of disseminating them to the National Health Service as a whole.

It would be no exaggeration to say that the total effect of all this work made a significant mark on national thinking about health service organization. At the end of the first nine years, contact had been made through conferences with senior health services staff from all over the country; a continuing dialogue had developed with a number of staff working within the Department of Health and Social Security itself; and shorter- or longer-lived field projects had been established in something of the order of twenty or thirty hospital or other health service sites.

In the field of social welfare services a similar range and intensity of work was achieved.[15] In 1969 a small team started social-analytic work in several Children's Departments in local authorities. Soon

[15] For published accounts *see* again Appendix B. In the pages that follow frequent reference will be made to the three fields of project-work just described: in industry (at the Glacier Metal Company), in the National Health Service and in local authority Social Services Departments. In particular, reference will frequently be made to several leading accounts mentioned in Appendix B of the detailed studies and findings in these three project fields, which will hereafter be identified only by their titles – *Changing Culture of a Factory* (Jaques, 1951); *Exploration in Management* (Brown, 1960); *Hospital Organization* (Rowbottom et al., 1973); and *Social Services Departments* (Brunel Institute of Organization and Social Studies, 1974).

the team was increased, and the scope was broadened to include the existing Welfare and Mental Health Departments, also part of local authorities. In a major nationwide reorganization in 1971 these three kinds of department were combined into a 'social services' department in each authority, whose brief was to deal with and to help prevent social distress of all kinds in children, problem families, the homeless, the elderly and mentally ill, and the disabled. By 1976, through conference work with senior officers, links had been established with about two-thirds of all the new Social Services Departments in the country. In addition, more or less intensive and continuous social-analytic projects had been established in about a dozen of these Departments.

Much of the social-analytic work in this second field centred around the problematic question of the intrinsic nature of social work and welfare work. Flowing from this were issues of how such work could best be controlled and supervised (assuming indeed that the very idea of specification and supervision was appropriate to the work). There was also the question of how the total activity with any particular client could best be planned and co-ordinated, and what distinct kinds or levels of professional or lesser skills might be brought to bear. This latter consideration naturally spread into questions of the identity of newly emerging professional groups, the distinctions between them, and the qualifications and training needed for each. How did qualified social workers differ from residential workers, or workers in day centres? What were the proper roles of occupational therapists, specialist teachers, family aides, home helps and so on, who were increasingly employed?

Another major concern, natural during this period, was the best form of overall departmental structure. Should the major departmental division be by kind of work, by geographical district, or by kind of client? Was a straightforward hierarchic structure appropriate to the work to be done and kind of people employed? If not, what was the alternative? If so, how many (or few) management levels were necessary? What sort of support and planning organization was necessary?

As Departments began gradually to get their immediate domestic concerns into some order they started to turn their attention to broader issues; and social-analytic work responsive as it is to the chief concern at any time of the people it works with naturally followed them. Thus later projects started to consider such things as the important links between social welfare, health services and education services, as a whole. The relationship of Social Services Departments

to the total corporate local authority enterprise, and to various voluntary bodies in the community also, came increasingly into view.

   By 1976 then, the social-analytic method had been applied in a
very considerable range of fields, and in respect of a very considerable variety of problems.

   It had been applied in industry, public services, central government and a number of smaller voluntary and charitable organizations. It had been devoted to very large-scale problems, such as the
reorganization of a huge national service, and to innumerable min-
ute ones. It had involved work with those close to the operational
front-line, like manual workers, technicians, clerical staff, salesmen,
nurses and social workers. It had been concerned with detailed
analysis of the basic work called for from various agencies in various
settings. It had been concerned with innumerable issues of organizational relationships and structure. It had been concerned with
questions of grading and pay, with industrial relations, staff
representative systems, and appeals procedures. It had been concerned with distinctions and definitions of newly emerging occupa-
tions and professions, and with clarification of the relations between
them.

# 2 An Illustrative Case-Study And Social Analysis Defined

In moving towards a more precise definition of social analysis as it has now become, it is helpful to prepare the ground by considering in some detail an actual case-study of a typical social-analytic project. This particular project was carried out in the course of the health services work described in the previous chapter.

## An Illustrative Case-Study – The Inter-relationships of Three Chief Officers in a Hospital Group

In November 1968 social-analytic work was started in the Hillingdon Hospital Group in West London. This consisted of one medium-sized general hospital and a number of smaller ones, all part of the National Health Service and all under the immediate control of an appointed governing body known as the Hospital Management Committee (HMC). In one of their early projects the Brunel team were invited by the three 'chief officers' of the Group to study their roles and relationships. The first of these was the Group Secretary who, besides acting specifically as secretary to the HMC, was described as the chief administrator and included under his direct control various 'service' departments like catering, housekeeping, portering, supplies, and personnel work. The second was the Chief Nursing Officer who, as the title implies, was the head of all the nursing and midwifery service. The third was the Treasurer. Aside from the medical consultants these were the three most senior staff in the Group.

One obvious question for these three officers – and one which could prove quite bothersome on occasion – was, who was the most senior of the three, and by how much? In many ways the Group Secretary undoubtedly had the edge, and occupied the highest-paid post. An existing organization chart depicted him clearly at the centre of all the Group staff and with a firm line proceeding from the HMC through him, and him only, to all other officers including the Treasurer and the Chief Nursing Officer. The latter, nevertheless, were shown as 'high' as he was on the chart, but not quite so centrally placed. (Organization charts are always fascinating, not so much for what they directly and clearly say, as for what they imply about the conscious or unconscious assumptions of those who draw them up – in this case the Group Secretary!)

This situation, though commonplace in the hospital service, as not without its tensions. Both the original Group Secretary and his successor who was appointed shortly after the start of the project, stressed the need for the HMC to have one officer, one 'chief executive', to see that their policies and decisions were implemented and that the total work of the Group was co-ordinated. The Treasurer, for his part, emphasized in discussion that the Group Secretary should be regarded only as a 'first among equals' and stressed the need to recognize his (the Treasurer's) own ultimate independence as a direct financial adviser to the HMC itself. For example, there were inevitably occasions when his view and the Group Secretary's view would diverge on what budgetary proposals for the coming year to lay before the HMC.

The Chief Nursing Officer stressed similar concern in discussion. She felt that there were times when her ability to establish direct communication with the governing body or its chairman on matters of vital concern to her, like nurse recruitment policy, were in danger of being blocked by the Group Secretary's attempts to get all matters for HMC attention in reasonable shape and under good control before submitting them. On the other hand, all three concurred with the view that any situation where chief officers were in regular and overt disagreement with each other during actual HMC meetings would be intolerable, both from the viewpoint of the officers and for that matter of the members too.

In exploring the exact quality of the roles to be played here it soon became very plain that neither a simple 'equal colleague' arrangement nor a straightforward 'superior-subordinate' (or 'managerial') arrangement (see Figure 2.1) was going to prove fitting or serviceable. Clearly some more complex patterns had to be considered.

In the Spring of 1970 the idea of a 'monitoring' relationship began to be explored, whose content might be summed up by the phrase –

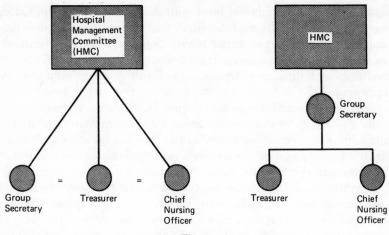

*Figure 2.1*

'check, discuss and (if need be) report'. It seemed clear, for example, that the Group Secretary had a monitoring function to perform not only in respect of explicit hospital regulations such as those governing employment, but in every area where established practices or common codes of acceptable work and good behaviour could be discerned. If one of his senior colleagues, or any other member of the group of hospitals (including doctors) suddenly went off the rails or grossly misbehaved, it would certainly be the Group Secretary's job to see that something was done about it. It was also clear that the Treasurer had what might readily be called a monitoring function to perform in respect of the rate at which money was spent in relationship to estimates and budgets, and in his auditing work in respect of the adequacy and propriety of actual accounting and cash-handling processes.

Over and above this, however, it seemed clear that there was some second and perhaps more crucial relationship at stake. It might perhaps be described as a 'coordinating' one. This would be like a managerial relationship in some respects, and in others decisively different. For example, it seemed necessary for the Group Secretary to carry a general co-ordinating role in implementing new HMC policies or in dealing with unexpected upsets. In doing this it was agreed that the Group Secretary would have to carry authority to make firm proposals for action, to arrange meetings, to obtain first-hand knowledge of progress on agreed projects and to decide what should be done in situations of uncertainty. However it did not feel appropriate that he should have authority in case of sustained dis-agreement with another chief officer to issue overriding instructions: that right should rest with the HMC. Nor should he have authority to make official appraisals of his colleagues' general performance, nor to bring sanctions to bear against them in the light of any such appraisals.

Exploration and analysis along these lines proceeded patiently but slowly – interrupted by other events and interspersed with other projects. Tentative ideas would to put forward by the social analyst on the basis of one discussion, only to be radically amended at the next. Gradually however, agreed formulations of 'monitoring' and 'co-ordinating' roles were produced, and a more complex statement of the desirable relationships of the three chief officers was defined in terms of them (Figure 2.2).

By early 1972 a first full statement of mutual roles and relation-ships was approved by the officers concerned, other senior staff, the HMC and the Regional Hospital Authority. It was agreed to 'test' it officially over a three-month period starting in May 1972.

At the end of this test period three further problems came to light and yet a further round of discussions commenced. One problem concerned the right of the Group Secretary to collate and edit reports and papers for the HMC. Necessary though this was, it was agreed that it must always be subject to the overriding right of the

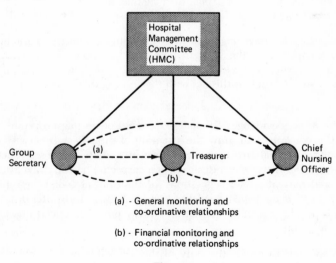

(a) - General monitoring and
    co-ordinative relationships

(b) - Financial monitoring and
    co-ordinative relationships

*Figure 2.2*

other chief officers to insist on submission of material as originally prepared where there were important differences of opinion on content or presentation which could not be resolved, if these other officers were truly to preserve their independence.

The second concerned the Treasurer's exact rights in controlling expenditure in his monitoring role. It had become evident that certain junior members of staff, like the nursing heads of small hospitals, had been in the habit of regarding the Treasurer's comments on particular items of excessive expenditure like high telephone bills as tantamount to executive instructions to cut costs, regardless of consequences. The principle was reaffirmed that responsibility for deciding when and where to spend money, even in excess of the budget, must rest with the particular manager of operational services concerned and ultimately with the HMC. However, it was also true that the Treasurer had a duty to monitor all expenditure, if necessary reporting shortcomings to the HMC itself. The following detailed procedure was agreed and adopted in order to reconcile these two principles:

The Treasurer is accountable for:
- monitoring for improper expenditure and improper financial procedures (i.e. outside law or regulations);
- monitoring for expenditure which appears excessive in its own right (e.g. excessive bills for individual items) even if encompassable within budget;
- monitoring the rate of expenditure against budget;
This *monitoring* relationship applies to all hospital and Group staff.

In each case his *monitoring* authority will include authority to obtain first-hand knowledge of the issue in point, and authority to persuade the officer concerned to modify his actions. In no case, however, will he have authority to instruct, as this lies with the accountable superior or superior body.

Where he sees evidence of *improper expenditure* or an inappropriate financial procedure he will draw the attention of the officer concerned to it, and under normal circumstances expect immediate response. Where *expenditure which is excessive in its own right* is suspected he will draw attention to it and may also offer suggestions for remedial action. Where he sees *adverse trends in expenditure in relation to budget* he will draw attention to it – discuss possible corrective action and advise on the financial implication of such action.

Thus in each case it is the duty of the Treasurer or his staff to draw attention to apparent deficiencies and to recommend corrective action if

any can be seen. However the Treasurer would not have authority to
issue outright instructions in any of these cases. He might continue to
press the matter with the officer concerned at his discretion but, if significant difficulties or major issues arise, he must refer the matter to the head
of the service concerned. Copies of any written communication to the
officer concerned would automatically be sent to the head of the service.
It would then be up to the head of the service to take what action he
considered appropriate. If the Treasurer were not satisfied with the
action taken he would refer the matter to the Group Secretary who
would act within his overall monitoring and co-ordinating role (as
defined). If the Treasurer were still not satisfied he could then, at his
discretion, refer the matter to the HMC.

The third problem centred on a specific complaint from the
Treasurer. Whilst it was true that he was always involved in any
explicit discussions of financial planning or control, there were many
policy discussions on other topics of which he remained ignorant, at
least to the stage where their financial implication came into view.
This was agreed to be unsatisfactory. The Treasurer should participate in all policy discussions if he was to do his job properly.
However within these discussions it would be his role to provide
financial suggestions, information and estimates. Firm decisions on
financial allocation must rest with officers accountable for the
provision of services, subject always to the final sanction of the
HMC.

This was not quite the end of the project. Immediate discussion
continued in respect of one particular point, namely the Treasurer's
exact strength of veto in cases of improper expenditure. However
other events were on the move. Planning was now beginning for the
reorganized health service which was to be introduced in 1974,
doing away with all hospital authorities and replacing them with
integrated health authorities. As it turned out this particular piece of
analytic work, together with other parallel studies, became of great
value in shaping general ideas about suitable management structure
in discussions at national level on detailed plans for the new service.

## Towards a Precise Definition of Social Analysis

This case-study illustrates many prominent features of social analysis
as it has now developed in practice. First and foremost it shows its
free-searching, exploratory nature – a continuing dialogue between
the actors in the situation and the analyst which follows the problems wherever they present themselves and for as long as is required.

We are not dealing here with any pre-planned or time-bounded study.

Often, though not always, this means long, intermittently active projects. The one described above stretched over three years in its various phases. However the pace of any project varies with the urgency of the problems faced. All depends on the priorities accorded by those directly involved.

The second point concerns the field of work, or subject matter. How natural it might have seemed to pick up discussion of the problems of relationship of these three actors in terms of their own personal attitudes to their jobs and to each other! In fact, although references to particular personalities were inevitably woven into preliminary discussions as may be imagined, the analysis itself was scrupulously concerned with structural matters, or what we shall wish to describe more precisely as social institutions. The issue is not: what is expected of William Smith in order that he develops a respectable personal relationship with John Brown? Rather, it is: what kind of activities are expected of this or any other Group Secretary in this situation, in respect of this or any Treasurer, in order that the system may continue to function properly, or to improve its function? (It may be supposed of course that one of the criteria of a well-designed organizational system will be its ability to facilitate satisfying personal relationships.)

Thirdly, there is no denunciation or exposure to be found here; no passionate advocacy, no whiff of revolution. What is to be seen instead is an evolutionary process based on a careful sensing of the existing situation, a teasing out of the knots and roughnesses, and a baring of the main strands and patterns. There is an underlying assumption that some sense, some degree of service, may be discovered in the existing social arrangements. The task is to distinguish these from other confusing and unserviceable elements with which they are interwoven. Since the subject matter under study is social relations, about which various assumptions on the part of the actors already exist, the process is one of clarification and definition rather than complete innovation. In the case-study described for example, the conceptions of monitoring and co-ordinating relationships may be thought of as having existed at some level all the time in that particular social situation. The job was to recognize them and bring them to clear consciousness; and then to make explicit trial of them. In the scrupulous study, exact definition, and subsequent test of such elements of social life we have another characteristic of social analysis, which is its scientific nature.

We may now summarize and generalize:

*Social analysis is an activity devoted to (1) gaining scientific understanding of, and thereby (2) facilitating enacted change in (3) social institutions, through (4) collaborative exploration by those actors immediately concerned in their working, and an independent analyst.*

Each of the four principal elements in this definition is independent, and each is necessary. It is possible to identify activities which are characterized by only two or three of these elements, but they constitute something distinctly different. For example, certain more sensitive kinds of management consultancy work may include the last three elements, but lack any genuine concern with generating, or even using, scientific theory or knowledge, relying instead on seasoned personal judgement about the wisest course to pursue in any given situation. Most so-called 'operational research' may be scientifically based, may be oriented to change, and may even employ collaborative exploration, but may simply not be concerned with social institutions. Much sociological or anthropological study may be concerned with gaining scientific understanding of social institutions, but not at all concerned with facilitating enacted change, at least not in the immediate situations under study.

Above all it must be stressed that social analysis is a scientific research activity. It is an activity dedicated to discovering and validating new scientific knowledge. Of course the knowledge must be viable and can only be tested by use, but in the end it is those with whom the analyst works, not the social analyst himself, who must bear the responsibility for implementing change.

Might social analysis be described then as applied research? All must depend here on what is intended by this phrase. Certainly social analysis is directly linked to immediately pressing social problems. However, it is not just concerned (as is much applied research) with providing by rigorous methods solutions to particular problems, and with that alone. On the contrary it is aimed at producing widely applicable generalizations. Indeed, it is an axiom of the method that it is precisely by attention to particular and individual social problems that the strongest chance of advancing general theory arises in the social sciences. In this context 'pure' and 'applied' are seen as unreal alternatives.

On the other hand, social analysis certainly comes within the bounds of 'action research', at least as it is defined in one leading statement – 'action research is any activity which aims to contribute both to the practical concern of people in an immediate problematic situation and to the goals of social science, by joint collaboration within a mutually acceptable ethical framework'.[1] (How far most existing action research actually manages to make a significant contribution to general scientific knowledge is, as has already been suggested, another matter.)

The chapters which follow are all concerned one way or another with exploring and elaborating the various elements in the precise definition of social analysis at which we have now arrived. The next two chapters attempt to complete the task of the first part of this book, which is to establish an understanding of the general nature of social analysis, by exploring more fully two basic conceptions which appear in the definition, the first that of 'enacted change in social institutions', and the second that of 'collaborative exploration'.

---

[1] Rapoport (1970), p. 499. (For further discussion of action research *see also* Foster (1972), *An Introduction to the Theory and Practice of Action Research in Work Organizations.*) Social analysis as defined here also comes within the broad conception of 'planned change' defined by Bennis, Benne and Chin (1970) as 'a conscious, deliberate and collaborative effort to improve the operations of a human system, whether it be self-system, social-system, or cultural-system through the utilization of scientific knowledge'; or various other similar conceptions, for example 'planned social intervention' as defined by Hornstein *et al.* (1971).

# 3 The Field of Work – Enactable Change in Social Institutions

Consider the three following situations, each drawn from real life, in which an outside social analyst was invited to help members of an organization to deal with their problems.

*Situation 1:* The problem arose in a unit of some twenty or thirty people who carried out test programmes on physical products of various sorts, and some straightforward research work of a similar kind. The unit was physically isolated and most of the staff had worked there for many years, so that a strong network of personal relationships and a powerful feeling of common social identity had grown. The initial statement of the problem pointed specifically to one person, the deputy head of the unit. This person had been the centre of a series of rows and upsets involving both his own chief and other staff, and stretching back over several years, indeed since the time of his internal promotion to the post over the heads of one or two more senior and highly paid colleagues. Should one proceed on the assumption that the most important thing on which to concentrate, was the individual centrally concerned himself? Should one try for example to discover or devise special training programmes to help him improve his personal ways of interacting with other people? Or should one consider ways of exploring more broadly the whole culture of the department as it generally affected attitudes, communications and interpersonal relationships in order to see if this particular instance was evidence of some deeper malaise? Or should one simply start by looking at various assumptions about the basic institutionalized roles involved, including what it meant to be a 'deputy'? Perhaps the problem stemmed from the conflicting interpretations given to this role and the authority it properly carried, by the various people in the situation, including the designated deputy himself and his chief.

*Situation 2:* The general problem posed was how to establish better processes of settling prices for individual products within a manufacturing company employed mainly in 'jobbing' production. Dozens or even hundreds of prices were being fixed every day by specialist estimators. Although there existed specific guidelines for their work, the general feeling was in the event that prices tended to drift up and down in an uncontrolled way. Not only was there lack of control under existing policies, but changes in pricing policies could not be implemented with any degree of certainty as to the result. Should one concentrate on improving things like the kind of cost or market data fed into individual calculations, or the actual formulae of calculation used? Or should one look at the broader issue of where authority for making various levels of decisions about prices was assigned amongst sales, accounting and other staff within the company: a look at the social or organizational aspects of the pricing process rather than the technicalities themselves?[1]

*Situation 3:* The general problem posed was that of the quality of 'intake' work in a children's welfare agency; that is, the work of making some initial response to a steady bombardment of requests for help in dealing with children in distress or trouble, homeless families and the like. It appeared that the section dealing with this intake work was overloaded. It was having difficulty in getting 'long-term' work-sections to accept referrals. Above all it was failing to act as it was intended to, as an effective control mechanism for the total workload of the agency.[2] Should attention be directed to helping to improve the detailed methods of assessing and responding to new applications; should one, that is, get into the actual technicalities of the so-called 'casework process'? Or should effort be concentrated on making a systematic survey of the various kinds of bombardment arising and their relative frequency, with a view to providing a better way of categorizing cases, and a more rational allocation of

[1] *See* Brown and Jaques (1964), *Product Analysis Pricing.* As it happened in fact, both these aspects of pricing were considered simultaneously in this particular project in the Glacier Metal Company.

[2] *See Social Services Departments,* Chapter 8.

resources and priorities? Or again, should attention be directed to deeper organizational issues, such as getting a clearer view of what precise function the intake section was supposed to be performing; what kind of monitoring, support, and guidance, the supervisor was expected to be providing to individual workers; and what exact procedures were appropriate for negotiating the transfer of cases to 'long-term' sections where continued work was called for?

Real-life problems in organized groups tend not to come in separate packages to which simple 'personal', or 'cultural', or 'technical', or 'planning', or 'organizational', labels can always be attached without hesitation. And if they appear at first sight to correspond directly to one of these categories, further exploration will often reveal accompanying or underlying issues of other kinds. Nevertheless, those independent agents who offer help in such situations cannot explore or pretend to explore everything in the same depth. Whilst being aware of other aspects and concerns, they must be clear about the extent and limits of their own field of competence. Often it is legitimate to examine in depth any one of a number of possible aspects of a problem. Each separate exploration, whether it be directed towards individual people and their personal interactions, the specific techniques of work, matters of planning and resource allocation, or general organization, may pay its own substantial dividends. Sometimes however the change-agent must recognize for himself, and make clear to those with whom he works, that the application of his own particular skill is not really what the situation requires.

In the case of social analysis, the chosen field of work is that of social institutions. Moreover, being concerned with a deliberate, scientific approach to change in social institutions, the focus is on what is *enactable* as regards such change. In exploring these statements further, let us start by considering more closely the general ideas of 'social institutions' and 'enactment'.

## Social Institutions and Enactment

All social life is conditioned by some things which are particular to the individuals in interaction at any point, and others which are general in that kind of interaction wherever or whenever it´ takes place. We shall take 'social institutions' to mean all those general aspects of the interactions in any society, large or small, which endure beyond changes in individual membership. Thus defined, they include for example all forms of government, all law, all established patterns of family life, marriage, occupation, economic exchange, all customs and all language. And in any smaller society within the larger – a particular local community, factory or hospital, say – they include as well whatever forms or customs are both lasting within it and particular to this smaller setting.[3]

Although from one point of view the various social institutions in society can be regarded as fixed and durable things, closer inspection will show that the whole vast framework is itself undergoing steady transformation and change, more or less rapid in its various parts. Much if not most of this change will be taking place in a spontaneous and unplanned way. In more self-conscious societies however, people will become increasingly aware of what is afoot, and will seek through their own individual actions to hasten change in social institutions here, or to inhibit or redirect it there. Issues such as the changing role of women in society, or the respective duties of spouses in marriage, may become matters of general and explicit discussion, in the course of which innumerable individuals may make up their own minds whether to resist or follow certain trends.

In some particular matters however, it will be felt possible and indeed desirable, not simply to leave things to spontaneous collective drift, based on innumerable individual changes in belief and attitude. It will be felt possible and desirable to make changes by *enactment*: that is, the deliberate introduction of change through public proclamation of explicit statements which are binding on all those in the particular society concerned, be it large or small.[4]

Law-making provides an obvious example of enactment. In such matters as how women are treated in employment, when growing children can be given independence, how far the environment may be altered by building or polluted by refuse, how money shall be raised for communal services, and innumerable others like them, we are not content simply to observe the gradual shift of customs and practice. It is felt necessary to lay down specific authoritative rules and standards which hold throughout the community. In advanced societies the need for some degree of law and regulation is felt in respect of practically every aspect of collective life.

Then there is the deliberate establishment of new associations of

[3] There is no standard or established definition of 'social institutions' in social theory. For a summary of various usages *see* Mitchell (1968), *A Dictionary of Sociology*.

[4] *See* the distinction made by the late nineteenth-century American sociologist, William Sumner, between 'crescive' social institutions, that is the main slowly changing body of customs, usages and mores in any society (which he also referred to collectively as 'folkways') on the one hand; and what he described as 'enacted social institutions' on the other: Sumner (1959), *Folkways*.

various kinds – recreational, commercial, occupational and so on – again so typical of modern society. Here too, beyond a certain stage, something more formal and explicit than the spontaneous inter-action of a group of interested individuals is required, and explicit constitutions are therefore enacted through such things as 'memor-anda of associations' and 'membership rules'.

Then again there is the deliberate establishment of executive organization to serve the purposes of such associations or the State itself. At first, in small undertakings, it is sufficient to employ a few paid assistants, volunteers, friends or relatives, all working together in an informal and uncharted manner. Beyond a certain stage of growth however, this will not do. The thing has to be 'organized'. Separate departments, divisions and sections are created, each with its own given functions. Specific posts and positions are designated, each with its own particular duties, requirements and rewards. Major changes do not just happen by chance. They are specifically enacted in official memoranda, circulars, organization charts and the like.

Seen like this, it is starkly apparent just how much of contempor-ary life is comprehended for better or worse by enacted organization. The great social change of the Western world from mediaeval to modern times has been a general movement away from the crescive social institution – the family, the tribe, the feudal system, the bonds-man, brother, servant and liege – towards the enacted social institu-tion – the company, the association, the statutory body, the em-ployee, the colleague and the contractor.[5]

## The Scope of the Potential Field of Social Analysis

As we have said, the chosen field of work of the social analyst is that of social institutions. However, it is also a fundamental characteristic of the work that it is concerned not just with generating better understanding of social institutions, but in helping to change them. And it is taken as axiomatic that if change is to be in any sense scientifically based, it must be capable of being stated in explicit terms so that all those who are going to be affected by it can under-stand exactly what it comprises. It follows that the concern of the

[5] *See* the general discussion of this major thread in nineteenth-century thought in Nisbet (1967), *The Sociological Tradition. See also* the comments on the same general theme in the context of the modern industrial setting, in Fox (1974), *Beyond Contract: Work, Power and Trust Relations.*

social analyst is not just with change in social institutions, but with enactable change.

It also follows that work can only be undertaken with groups of people who have the collective ability to undertake deliberate or enacted change in their own social institutions; that is, within what would usually be described in present-day terminology as 'organizations' of some kind. Nevertheless, this still presents an extremely wide field of potential work. It ranges from the modern State considered as a complex undertaking in its own right at one extreme, to a small club or society at the other. It includes such diverse undertakings as businesses, churches, trade unions and voluntary associations. In the case of the State it encompasses not only the civil-service bureaucracies or other executive arms, but the full legislative and judicial machinery as well. In the case of voluntary associations or companies of various kinds it includes the prime membership themselves and any governing council or committee structure in addition to the officers or employees.[6]

In practice much work is likely to be with the leaders of such groups – the appointed or elected officers of associations, the managers or directors of private concerns, the governors and senior staff

[6] Finding the correct general label here is difficult. 'Organization' seems the most suitable even though it might be seen as possessing implications of intrinsic and invariable hierarchic structure, or super-large size – implications which are both in fact undesired in this context. 'Association' as an alternative is too narrow a term in some ways and too broad in others. Paid employees for example, who might certainly regard themselves as members of 'an organization', would not necessarily however see themselves as members of an 'association'. On the other hand, the word association can be used legitimately of, say, a marriage or a small partnership where no question arises of enacted change of internal institutional forms themselves. 'Bureaucracies' or 'bureaucratic organizations' is far too limiting. As we have just said 'organization' is intended to include such things as the prime membership of voluntary associations and their elected governing bodies, neither of which could be suitably described as 'bureaucratic' even if they are formally enacted or constituted. (*See* here Jaques' important distinction of associations from the bureaucratic employment systems which they commonly create – Jaques (1976), *A General Theory of Bureaucracy*.) Moreover, there is no reason to suppose that even employment systems must be invariably bureaucratic in form, in the classical sense defined by Weber (Gerth and Mills, 1948, *From Max Weber*). The only bounding considerations for potential social-analytic work are (a) that the group concerned is permanent enough to have developed its own institutional forms, and (b) that it is large or complex enough to warrant making explicit statements or enactments about the institutions which are to prevail.

For further discussion of these definitional problems *see* MacIver and Page (1950), *Society: An Introductory Analysis*; Etzioni (1964), *Modern Organizations*; and Jaques (1976), op. cit.

of public undertakings – as these are usually the people most acutely conscious of the needs for clear social arrangements, and also in an authoritative position to change them. But it can also be done (and has in fact also been) with the less powerful in any setting: for example with groups of shop-floor workers who wish to associate and organize for their own protection or in pursuit of their own interests.

On the other hand, the scope for work with what might be referred to loosely as the 'customers' of organizations is often in principle more limited. The criticism has sometimes been levelled at social analysis that it fails to take direct account of the views and needs of, say, patients in hospitals, or the so-called clientele in social work. In fact there is no difficulty in working with such people if two conditions are met. The first is that they have some ability for collective action: that they have already formed some sort of voluntary association or pressure group. The second is that they should seek assistance. Considerable social-analytic work has been undertaken for example with members of 'community health councils' whose specific brief is to represent the local interests of the consumer in health matters.

However if consumers, customers or clientele, are not already organized into groups of some form or other, there is little that the social analyst himself can do. The people concerned simply do not have at this stage the ability (or perhaps the willingness) to develop their own social institutions. There may be work here for the community worker or the political activist. There may be potential work for the social surveyor in undertaking systematic reviews of the incidence of need, or of responses to existing facilities and services. But there is no work at this point for the social analyst.

However, it must not be assumed that this inherent restriction to working only with members of organized groups themselves necessarily dictates an inward-looking approach. The social analyst frequently spends much time and effort helping those with whom he is working to define better what sorts of services they ought to be providing to the outside world. Indeed as we shall see later, in any prolonged or intensive work with members of an organized body, a searching analysis of the basic *functions* which that body should be performing in relation to its broader social setting is in the end the most important and fundamental issue at stake. In addition, the social analyst will often find himself helping organizations to develop specific institutional forms which will allow them to relate better to the society they serve – better social- or market-research sections, better selling or marketing departments, better complaint-handling procedures and so on.

**Enactable Features of Social Institutions**

So far we have established that social analysis is concerned with changes in social institutions. Moreover it is concerned with changes that can be explicitly specified and deliberately introduced, in other words with enactable changes. This means that it can only be employed where the people concerned have in principle the possibility of undertaking enacted change; that is, in organized social activities of various kinds.

The next step is to consider more closely what enactments of social institution actually look like. It seems that there are only a limited number of basic forms which they can in fact take.

(1) For a start, enactments may be made about the *structure and composition* of organized bodies in terms of the various positions that are to exist, their titles, and the way they are to be linked. For example (for a voluntary society) 'there shall be a governing committee consisting of six members, one of whom shall be chairman, one the secretary and one the treasurer'; or (for a public welfare agency) 'the plan is to have five operating divisions geographically based; they will be supported by headquarters sections dealing with research and planning, development, training and administration'.

(2) Enactments may be made about the *aims to be pursued* or *function to be carried out* by those in specific positions, or in specific groups. For example, 'the aim of the organization is to prevent and alleviate social distress in individuals, families and communities', 'the function of the operating division is to provide a comprehensive range of social services throughout a given geographical area, of the kind approved and financed by the department'; 'the duties of the shop-steward include that of collecting dues from union members, and of communicating union views and policies to members; also that of acting as a spokesman and representative for all members of the shop in dealings with the particular employer and his agents'; 'the function of the community health council is to act as a mouthpiece for community views of the quality of existing services, and also to contribute a community view in planning'.

(3) Enactments may be made about the *authority* attaching to various positions: 'the committee has authority to authorize expenditure up to a maximum of £500 . . .'; 'the social worker has authority to receive children into care where . . .'; 'the departmental manager has authority to assign work to his subordinates, assess results, appraise personal performance and recommend any subsequent action called for . . .'; 'the head of the medical division has authority to call

meetings, and to issue proposed programmes of action within unanimously approved policy . . .'.

(4) Enactments may be made about the *accountability* attaching to various positions: 'the Area Nursing Officer is directly accountable to the Area Health Authority'; 'the employees' representative is accountable to those who elected him'. (Note however that statements of accountability *for*, as opposed to statements of accountability *to*, are merely statements in another form of duties or responsibilities, that is, of functions to be carried out as described in (2) above.)

(5) Enactments may be made about the *rewards and perquisites* attaching to any position: 'the post carries a salary of . . .'; 'a free car is provided . . .'; 'officers of Grade 3 or above will travel first class. . .'. (Here perquisites must be taken to include various signs of status or prestige, and not just things of economic worth.)

(6) Finally, a variety of enactments may be made about the standards, prohibitions or protocol to be observed in various social situations: what may be generalized as *rules and procedures* to be followed. There are examples here about the way in which various positions are to be filled: 'the two medical representatives are elected by members of the district medical committee'; 'all posts must be advertised internally before being offered in the open market'; 'a recognized engineering qualification is required'. There are examples of the way working interactions are to be pursued: 'unanimous agreement is required amongst the team before plans can be put into action'; 'if the recipient of a staff-officer's instructions, having discussed them with the staff-officer, is still in fundamental disagreement with them, then he and the staff-officer concerned should refer the matter to their common superior'; 'the constitution of the association may only be amended in general meeting, and by a majority of two-thirds of those present'. And there are innumerable other examples in such things as detailed procedures of election, or procedures for dismissal from post, or promotion procedures, or appeals or grievance procedures, or negotiation procedures – that is, not only statements of rules but statements of the steps by which rules are legitimately changed.

Although social analysis may be applied to the widest variety of organized social activities, it appears then that any enactments of change in social institutions which follow will always be in one or other of these six forms just identified. It appears that the end-products of social-analytic work, at least as far as specifically identified possibilities for enacted change are concerned, will be in terms of these six kinds, and these only.

Do these very terms like 'authority', 'accountability' and 'rules' seem to carry implications of what might be thought of as bureaucratic, formalized or hierarchical systems? It is important to recognize that the words are actually neutral, descriptive ones, and do not in fact carry any particular ideological burden, nor implications of any preferred organizational forms. If enactment of any kind is to take place, these or closely similar terms are all that is available to frame the various results required, whatever these may be. These terms would have to be employed equally in systematic enactments of the social structure of the most egalitarian, free-developing commune or kibbutz, as they would for the most highly marshalled factory system or authoritarian State bureaucracy.

Having said all this however, it is obviously the case that there are significant aspects of social institutions where direct enactment is impossible or inappropriate. Moreover there are many further aspects still of organized activity that do not even come within the general ambit of 'social institutions', that are nevertheless of interest and importance. A brief review now of some of these various other aspects of organized life will serve two purposes at this point. First, it will help to establish more firmly the idea of enactable aspects of social institutions by showing what this excludes as well as what it includes. Secondly, it will pave the way for showing how propositions about enacted change in social institutions may be systematically linked to other and deeper features.

## Other Aspects of Organized Activity Which May be Studied

What other aspects of organized social activity may be the subject of explicit study; other, that is, than enacted social institutions?

For a start it is clear that there are a whole host of *technical* issues which may arise in organized activity which may be the subject of explicit study. The phrase 'technical issues' obviously comprehends such matters as how certain kinds of products can best be manufactured, or sold, or certain data-processing operations carried out, certain crops grown, or certain diseases treated. We should be careful to include here as well, however, matters to which the word 'technology' with its immediate image of machinery and circuitry might not seem at first thought to apply so readily: how children are best brought up or educated, how training or psychotherapy is best carried out, how performance at work is best appraised and so on. (Nevertheless, there is a line between any such person-oriented technologies and general rules or procedures for regulating the relationships of various actors involved, which as we have seen, form part of a comprehensive statement about social institutions. Thus, the particular method by which the teacher trains his pupils to read is a matter of educational technology; but the authority relations between the two and any established modes of address and questioning from pupils to teachers are part of the established social institutions of schools.)

Apart from technical issues, there are what (following Brown[7]) may be described in general as *programming* matters. The broadest conception of 'programming' includes all those aspects of human affairs concerned with the specific goals, the specific sequences of action, and the specific time-tables to be pursued in various situations. In the industrial sphere it includes such subjects as 'corporate planning', 'production planning and control', 'stock control' and the quantitative aspects of market research. In the public sphere it includes such topics as 'planning programming budgeting' and 'cost benefit analysis'. The language of programming is the language of objectives and targets, of budgets and schedules, of time-scales, of relative priorities. It is a natural field for quantification, and there is much scope within it for various kinds of factual study and survey in order to establish the extent and range of needs, and how far they have been met. In terms of professional specialities, it is the realm of the economist, the statistician and the operational researcher. In the public sphere, it is the field of a certain kind of applied social researcher who is often also an advocate of particular social policies, using the data he gathers to support his case.

Beyond this lie many other aspects of organizational life which may be the subject of special attention. There may be study for example at the personal or psychological level – in terms of individual interests, attitudes, concerns, motivations, abilities and development. There may be study at what may be called the socio-

[7] *See Exploration in Management*, Chapter 11; also Brown and Jaques (1965a, 'Management Teaching', pp. 169–70. Brown lays much stress on the idea that all organizational work has three basic 'dimensions' – the 'personnel', the 'technical' and the 'programming': arguing indeed that these form natural and logical bases for the establishment of specialist or staff-officer roles in any organization. It may be noted that his conception of 'personnel' includes (and this is unusual) explicit concern with developing organization, i.e. social institutions, as well as other more conventional matters. Whilst considering attempts to conceptualize the various dimensions of organizational life, note may also be taken of an often quoted analysis by Leavitt (1965). This distinguishes 'task', 'people', 'technological' and 'structural' variables. Rough equivalences may perhaps be assumed between 'task' and 'programmes' and 'structure' and 'social institutions'.

psychological level, in terms of specific encounters, interactions and networks; the ephemeral groups that form and dissolve; the shifting communication patterns that follow; the roles (in basic terms like 'leader', 'conciliator', 'scapegoat') that particular individuals attract to themselves in relation to other individuals; the particular alliances or sub-groups that form; the dominant tone at any time, whether one of cooperation or conflict; of work or flight from work, of trust or mistrust and so on. As occasions change and individual members change, so do the forms of these particular aspects of social life, and in this sense they are transient or ephemeral.[8]

At a deeper level, organizational life may be studied in terms of the general culture which prevails and the stratification of power and status. One of the strongest trends in organizational studies of the last few decades has been towards what might be described as the study of general organizational *texture* – how 'bureaucratic' it is, how 'formalized' or 'complex'; how internally 'differentiated' or 'integrated', whether 'organic' or 'mechanistic' in general nature and so on.[9]

## The Relation of Study and Enacted Change

Life within organized groups may be studied then at a great variety of levels. Indeed, there are as many ways of studying life within organized social groups as there are of studying human society as a whole. Moreover, there are hardly any kinds of study which cannot in some way or other be made to yield a potential for change. The simple fact of making the actual members aware of the results of studies, however abstract or recondite, may always exert some degree of influence on their future views and behaviour in the setting concerned.

Now, getting change in general is one thing. Getting enacted change however, is quite another. Thus reporting to organizational

[8] It has already been noted in the first chapter how far the 'Organization Development' (OD) movement, indeed the whole 'action research' tradition has leaned in practice to a socio-psychological approach. Most of the leading figures from Lewin onwards have in fact been social psychologists by discipline – Bennis, Likert, Schein, Argyris, Blake and others. In viewing this situation, Bennis for one comments on the urgent need for OD practitioners to consider 'structural' issues as well as 'people' variables, but recognizes that very little of this has happened in fact (Bennis, 1969, p. 80).

[9] Starting with Burns' and Stalker's study of 'organic' and 'mechanistic' organizations (Burns and Stalker, 1961), a clear link can be seen, for example, with the work of Woodward (1965); Pugh, Hickson and various associates (1963, 1968, 1969); Lawrence and Lorsch (1967); and Hage and Aiken (1970).

members, surveys of their own attitudes or feelings, or facing them with their own actual behaviour in groups (a favourite tactic in 'OD' work), may cause some kind of change, but it is not in itself explicit, controlled or testable, change. Undertaking 'textural' studies may suggest that an 'organic' organization is more relevant, or more profitable, in some given conditions of market and technology, than a 'mechanistic' one, but any deliberate movement towards the one and away from the other will necessarily involve some explicit reallocation of function, redistribution of authority and restructuring of procedure.

Conversely, of course, there are some things which enacted change can never reach. Enactments may be made about specific aims or functions to be pursued, but the values or ideologies actually subscribed to by various individuals or groups is beyond the possibility of being changed in this way. Enactments may be made about the authority people carry, but none may be made directly about the power or influence they wield, or the degree of leadership they exhibit. Accountability may be assigned, but the sense of responsibility which gives it substance in practice is not a matter which can be enacted. Perquisites and status signs may be distributed at will, but personal esteem can only be won by individual performance.

Whether or not changes in such things as basic culture, outlook, or attitude are more important than specific enactable change is a perennial and perhaps unanswerable question. On the one hand, it may be suspected that enacted change which is not accompanied by some underlying shift in attitude and value will often be more a change in the letter than in the fact. On the other hand, it often seems that attempts to change values and attitudes directly without the firm guide of accompanying enactment are like one-night evangelical missions whose effects begin to fade even as the tents are being taken down the following day. However (to repeat the point), scientific change in social affairs, if there is to be any at all, can only take place through deliberate, explicit enactment.

We have already established the half-dozen or so aspects of social institutions that can in principle be the subject of enacted change. To these we may now add two further and different fields of potential enactment in their own right – collective *technologies* to be employed and collective *programmes*. It seems then, that enactable change may in principle be undertaken in three aspects of collective human activity: in social institutions, in technologies, and in programmes. In social analysis we are, of course, specifically interested in the first.

## The Impact of Other Aspects of Organized Activity on Enacted Social Institutions

We have indicated that social analysis is concerned with changes of a specific kind: enactable changes in social institutions. We have also established that there are many other aspects of organized activity that may be the subject of study and change. Although the social analyst is not concerned with the pursuit of change in these other things this does not for a moment mean that he can ignore them. On the contrary the relation between enacted institutional change and these other things is of greatest interest to him. Indeed, the explicit spelling out of the relationships between the two is, as we shall see, central to the work. A closer analysis of the essential nature of such statements of relationship between social institutions on the one hand, and various other given features and requirements on the other, is a task left until Chapter 8. So too is the demonstration of the possibility of casting such statements in a form which is both usable and scientific. For the moment some brief illustrations can be given of the kind of linkages which are under constant consideration.

There has for example been a strong concentration in social-analytic thinking on links between social institutions and the fundamental structure and distribution of human abilities. Questions like the following have been posed and explored. How are authority relationships in general, and more particularly those that involve the assessment of one person's performance and capabilities by another, possible or defensible without some accompanying idea of distinctively different levels of human ability? Are there discrete jumps in levels of general human ability to undertake organized work effectively? If so, what are its implications for the number of levels which it is possible to sustain generally in hierarchic organizations? Is it possible to carve out as many levels as we like in such situations, or are we limited in some definite way by the very raw material of human nature, as it were? [10]

Then there has been a continuous interest since the earliest days in the effect of emergent power-groups in society on social institutions. What sort of institutions are needed within an industrial setting to take account of the power of various groups of shop-floor workers to bring production to a halt if they so chose? What sort of institutions, 'work councils', 'appeals procedures' and the like, can give due

---

[10] See Jaques (1965a), 'Speculations Regarding Level of Capacity' and (1965b), 'A Preliminary Sketch of a General Structure of Executive Strata'; also Jaques (1976), *A General Theory of Bureaucracy*, Part 3.

means of expression to this power, without a constant series of stoppages on the one hand, or the complete undermining of executive authority on the other?[11]

The effects of more ephemeral groupings, networks and relationships – what has been referred to above broadly as 'socio-psychological aspects' – are always of concern to the social analyst. Transient social structure and deeper institutionalized structure always interact. Indeed, the way that transient patterns are tending to crystallize may often suggest the urge towards some new institutional form. Thus, one published report[12] describes a project with a large group of social workers who had just started to meet together in a newly formed Social Services Department in order to explore their general concerns about the way the Department was developing, and thereafter in some way, to communicate these general concerns to the senior managers of the Department. One of the things to which attention was drawn in the course of social analysis was the way in which certain institutionalized roles were tending to emerge and form spontaneously out of the meetings. One was the 'chairman' or the leadership role in the conduct of the meetings themselves. Another was the 'representative' role of communicating the feelings and suggestions of social workers to senior management, and relaying their responses. Problems were being experienced in sorting out who was to carry out such work on each occasion, and also of getting sufficient continuity. Inevitably, issues of differences in individual capabilities in performing such work arose as well.

Sometimes by contrast it is the very failure to develop satisfactory transient groupings and relationships day by day which may indicate faults in the explicit institutions which already exist. Good social institutions, it may be agreed, should be such as to encourage and facilitate satisfying and productive personal relationships. Thus, in the case-study described in the previous chapter it was the complaints of a *particular* group of hospital chief officers about difficulties in working together that formed the impetus for, and the starting point of, exploration. The problem was not seen, initially at least, as one of ambiguous or ill-defined institutional forms, but in terms of the difficulties of making easy, flexible relationships with particular colleagues in a wide range of situations of mutual interaction.

Many other different sorts of linkages have emerged in the course

[11] Jaques (1951), *Changing Culture of a Factory,* Chapter 10; Brown (1960), *Exploration in Management,* Chapter 17; and Brown (1971), *Organization,* Part 2.

[12] *Social Services Departments,* pp. 225–35.

of social-analytic work: the effect of geography on social institutions where staff are required to work on a site which is remote from the remainder of their colleagues in the same section or department for example; [13] the effect of the type of service demanded, as for example where nurses are required to provide continuous service around the clock in a hospital ward; [14] the effect of resource availability where for example, modified forms of organization have to be adopted because of lack of staff. [15] (The total range of needs and circumstances which may bear on institutional design are considered more fully in Chapter 8.)

## A Wider View of Possibilities for Enacted Change

It is not then that social analysis purports to ignore features of organized activity other than enactable aspects of social institutions. On the contrary, drawing links between particular institutional models and other variables such as personal capacity, professionalism, types of service demanded, geographical considerations and various other given circumstances and requirements is at the very heart of the scientific endeavour of social analysis. The point, to repeat it, is that social analysis is not itself directly concerned with *change* in these other variables – with developing individuals, improving personal relationships, changing technology, determining more relevant programmes and so on.

Generally, we may view the various possibilities for systematic study and enacted change in organized activity as shown in Figure 3.1. As we have said, enacted changes of three kinds are possible in principle: in social institutions, in technologies, or in programmes. If rational change is undertaken in any one of these areas it will need to be related to various deeper needs and circumstances which can be taken as 'givens'. The aim of study and analysis will be to elucidate these basic features, and to trace the linkages to possible enacted change. Moreover, any one basic feature may have implications in any of the three possible fields of change. Consideration of possible programmes or possible institutions may lead back to the same root-question of social or political values. Consideration of possible technologies or institutions may lead to the same basic issue of the nature of human capacities and skills, say, or the social struc-

[13] *See* the concept of 'outposting' in *Hospital Organization*, Chapter 4.
[14] See *Hospital Organization*, Chapter 7.
[15] *See* the case-study of the provision of social work in hospitals described in Chapter 8.

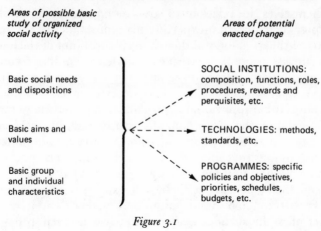

*Figure 3.1*

ture of the given environment. Conversely, any one basic feature of the social situation – say the emergence of some new kind of social problem in public services, or of some new potential market in industry – may suggest the need not only for new programmes of response, but for the development of new organizational institutions to administer such programmes, and the development too of new technologies of provision. And not only will technologies, programmes and institutions grow from the same common soil, but they will intertwine and interact at innumerable points thereafter.

## Social Institutions as a Legitimate Field of Study and Change in Its Own Right

Given this common root and close intertwining of institutions with both programmes and technologies, what brief has the social analyst to limit himself to studying the first only? One obvious answer is that he does so because he chooses to: because the subject interests him. It is only by such deliberate choices and restriction that adequate expertise and specialist knowledge can be developed. (As will be discussed more fully in due course, social analysis demands its own very considerable reservoir of specialist knowledge, apart from what special skills are required for effective social-analytic practice.) The impossibility need hardly be argued in relation to modern society of attempting to be expert in all possible aspects of social study or intervention, or even for that matter, in all possible aspects in relation to a particular object of study such as the human individual, the family, the work-institution or the community. Indeed, any who offer themselves in relation to any individual or group as the all-purpose scientist-cum-expert-helper must invite the greatest suspicion of the soundness of their judgement, if not of their probity.

Nevertheless there is a frequent tendency in those concerned professionally with helping to achieve change within organizations to believe that their particular field of expertise is the only one of any significant general applicability and validity. Applied mathematicians tend to enlarge the definition of 'operational research' until it becomes synonymous with any scientific approach to organizational problems. Social psychologists dub their approach 'organization development', and in using such a general term half-persuade themselves and their clients that their skill extends to all eventualities. Even 'work study' and 'organization and methods', at a very different level of sophistication, become stretched as their titling easily allows, to another kind of universal licence and qualification. In fact, it is never possible to comprehend social systems in their entirety, let alone to change every aspect at once. Specific fields of study and change emerge because they do contain some definite unity within them, because they do reveal definite boundaries with other nearby fields, and above all, because experience shows that undertaking changes within the field concerned, and without simultaneous changes in other matters, does in practice prove possible and useful.

Social institutions constitute such a field. It is not always necessary or practical to alter programmes or technologies every time some institutional change is made, or vice versa. Moreover, the field is a neglected one, which is strange in an increasingly organized society. At any rate, it has tended to be neglected below the level of the State as a whole, that is, below the level of the theory of political constitution and the law. For some reason – perhaps historical chance – both investigators of, and interventionists in, the smaller-scale organizations that abound in our society have tended to concentrate on other, more colourful and dramatic things: the interplay of personalities and power; the clash of outlooks and cultures; the introduction of new technologies; the mathematical bravura of quantitative analysis and 'scientific' resource allocation. By contrast, social analysis is concerned with the relatively undramatic: the sober statement of functions to be performed, of procedures to be observed, of authority, accountability and the like. And yet without the clear understanding of these things – the careful preparation of the stage as it were – the drama loses its cohesion and the interplay is in danger of dissolving in formless confusion.

# 4 The Idea of Collaborative Exploration

One of the apparent puzzles about social analysis is the absence of any of the more obvious manifestations of scientific activity – questionnaires, data sheets, computer tabulations, sample surveys, control groups and the like – in spite of its claims to scientific status.

In this chapter we shall show how social analysis, like certain other activities concerned with helping people towards a better understanding of the nature of their own problems and needs in particular situations, makes obligatory a radically different approach from that usually considered normal or standard in social science. This will be marked as the difference between 'collaborative exploration' and what may broadly be called 'objective study'. It will be noted that certain restrictions follow if collaborative exploration is adopted. However, attention will be drawn to the major scientific advantages which accrue, in terms of improved access to study situations, and the greatly increased commitment of all involved to get to the true nature of the matters at issue.

We shall see that where collaborative exploration is concerned with social institutions as in 'social analysis' (in contrast to other things to which the same approach might be applied) the wide-scale gathering of factual data does not usually turn out to be of great relevance. However, as will be shown in the chapters that follow, this does not at all imply that genuine scientific research ' is prohibited or that there need be any loss of scientific rigour, generality or objectivity.

## Problems of Describing Social Institutions

Let us start by considering some of the special problems that arise whenever any attempt is made to make a systematic exploration or study of social institutions, as such.

Consider, for example, a discussion that might be held with a number of senior social workers about the general nature of their roles as leaders of teams of social workers, social work assistants and trainees in some local office of a social welfare agency. Let us suppose that four senior social workers are involved – Miss A, Mr B, Miss C and Mrs D. The discussion turns to one particular aspect of their work – supervision of team members. Miss A says that she makes a practice of having regular supervision sessions with her trainees and assistants, but leaving the social workers themselves to approach her at their own initiative if they have work problems to discuss. Mr B observes that this is not the case for most seniors, who, like him, try as far as possible to arrange regular supervision sessions with social workers as well as with the others. Miss C then breaks in, drawing attention to a memorandum from the director of the department. This quite clearly describes senior social workers as 'in charge' of teams, and 'responsible for keeping a regular check on all the work done'. Surely this means checking on the work of social workers as well as the others, she argues. At this point Mrs D darkly observes that there is far too much talk of supervision and checking in social work. Any 'decent' professional social worker should be able to get on with his own work. She herself would like to see the senior grade, which is currently tied closely to administrative responsibilities, kept simply as a means of giving higher pay to more experienced practitioners.

Quite regardless of the possible merits of various viewpoints, it is clear that the argument is being conducted at a number of different levels. Miss A and Mr B are describing their individual perceptions or assumptions about the roles of team leaders as they are currently played. Miss C is talking about an official statement of the team leaders' role, which may or may not have affected the working assumption that people make in practice. And Mrs D is on quite a different tack: she is addressing herself to how the role ought to be conceived if things were as they should be, and quite regardless of what, in practice, it is taken to be at present.

In social-analytic thinking these levels have been distinguished as the 'manifest', the 'assumed' and the 'requisite'.[1] The terms can be

[1] *Exploration in Management*, Chapter 2.

applied equally to any enactable aspect of social institutions: to functions to be performed, authority, procedures to be observed, expected role and so forth. *Manifest* statements of any aspect of social institutions are those which carry a stamp of authority by virtue of coming from some 'higher' level, or by virtue of having received some general and formal sanction. They are the official enacting statements.[2] Such statements have their own reality, but whether or how far they are observed in practice is a matter for exploration. Another kind of 'reality' is comprised by the various perceptions of different individual actors in the situation. Since these are more than just idle perceptions but are adopted in fact by each person concerned as his own basis for action and interaction, they are aptly described as *assumed* views or statements of social institutions. That people's assumptions of the nature of their roles vary from those with whom they interact, or even from those in similar positions, is a fact that is re-demonstrated in practically every piece of social-analytic exploration carried out.[3] On the other hand, there is clearly some shift in argument when the discussion moves from existing assumptions to what ought to be the case if things were differently and better arranged – what in social analysis has been dubbed the *requisite* situation.[4]

Clearly, in undertaking discussions such as those described above, it is very difficult to talk in any straightforward sense about 'collecting the facts'; the facts, that is, of the social institutions at work. Nor is it any use attempting to revert to direct observation. Social institutions cannot be directly observed. All that can be observed is people's overt behaviour. From this the external observer may make his own inferences about what is implied beneath, but only at some considerable risk.

Suppose, for example, that an attempt is made to observe the institutions prevailing in a group of hitherto unknown people in

[2] This is very close to Robert Merton's well-known conception of the 'manifest functions' of any social institution. However, there is more of a problem with his complementary conception of 'latent functions'. He defines these as 'objective consequences which are unintended' (Merton, 1968, *Social Theory and Social Structure*, Chapter 3). But who is in a position to make such 'objective' interpretation, and to decide that these represent the 'real' functions? Is it the omniscient social scientist? What of the assumptions of various other actors in the situation?

[3] *See* similar findings in Gross *et al.* (1957), *Exploration in Role Analysis: Studies of the School Superintendent Role*; and Kahn *et al.* (1964), *Organizational Stress: Studies in Role Conflict and Ambiguity*.

[4] Exactly what is implied in the concept of 'requisite' is explored in detail in the chapters that follow, particularly in Chapters 5 and 8.

discussion together in some work setting. It may be noted that one individual takes the lion's share of the discussion. Does this mean that he is the leader? In some sense he obviously is, at least at that moment; but he is not necessarily the person who occupies the established position of authority as head of the group. Maybe that person is sitting back, and reserving for the moment his crucial approval or veto. Maybe his own personal style of leadership is for the most part a relatively passive one. Overt behaviour, signs of emotion or conflict, indications of dominance or passivity, may be directly observed. But the functions people are expected to provide in particular positions, the nature of the rights and duties associated with those positions, or the norms and customs which are supposed to condition interaction between those positions may not.

So in order to understand these latter things better one must enter into questioning or discussion. And then, as noted above, it will almost certainly be discovered that there is no definite consensus on what exists amongst the actors concerned. Whatever the institution being discussed – not only the substance of a particular position in an organization but even such things as the nature of various family roles, or the proper form of some common social usage – there are likely to be a variety of differences in perception and view, ranging from subtle to gross.

Moreover, in the course of exploring and clarifying individual assumptions, the process of the exploration itself cannot help but modify the views of those whose institutions are being explored. The researcher (assuming that there is one) inevitably finds himself contaminating, as it were, the very purity of the substance he wishes to isolate.

Nevertheless, having stressed the uncertain, shifting status of many features of social institutions, it must now be added that there are other features which do at any time have a clear unequivocal existence. Social institutions do in varying degree have some definite reality, independent of the view of any individual. Had we asked the social workers above for example, to which office they belonged, they would no doubt have replied swiftly and without doubt or dissent. Certainly (they might say) an area office exists, regardless of what debate there might be about its exact functions in the community. Certainly a number of teams exist, each with its leader, regardless of what debate there might be about the exact role to be played by this leader. Thus, any one aspect or characteristic of a particular social institution may be tolerably clear, agreed and valid at any given time, whilst other aspects of the same institution may be unclear or contentious.

At this point, the paradoxical nature of social institutions has to be recognized and faced. Speaking generally, it is true that social institutions are transient things, ever-changing in the light of new perceptions of need and circumstance. And at the same time it is true they have the unchanging character of given realities; of social 'facts'. They are by their nature 'givens' for men who must observe them, and they are also the creation of those same men or their predecessors. Sometimes it is fruitful to view them one way and sometimes the other.[5]

In previous social-analytic writing this situation, it may be suggested, has not hitherto been clearly recognized. It is true that a fourth level of description of social institutions has regularly been invoked, the *extant*. This fourth level has been defined as 'the situation as revealed by systematic exploration and analysis'.[6] But this is not quite the same thing as a straightforward factual view of social institutions (where this is admissible). If any 'systematic exploration and analysis' is necessary, for example to establish whether area offices or departments, or other units exist, their existence could hardly be said to be a matter of unequivocal fact! (Not surprisingly, clear distinctions between 'assumed' and 'extant' statements, as just defined, have proved extremely difficult to establish in practice in actual project work.) 'Extant' might, as it happens, be a good term to express the straightforward factual aspect of social institutions, but in view of its rather different definition in previous social-analytic literature, it might well be confusing to use it in this way. We shall therefore continue to distinguish this other view of social institutions by phrases such as 'factual', 'straightforward' or 'unequivocal'.

At this point brief account may be taken of the ideas of 'formal organization' and 'informal organization' often employed in the literature on organization. Straightforward though such a distinction may appear at first glance, further consideration reveals profound ambiguities.

---

[5] *See* Berger and Luckman (1967), *The Social Construction of Reality*. As they summarize their thesis: 'Durkheim tells us: "The first and fundamental rule is: *consider social facts as things*." And Weber observes: "Both for sociology in the present and for history, the object of cognition is the subjective meaning complex of action." These two statements are not contradictory. Society does indeed possess objective facticity. Any society is indeed built up by activity that expresses subjective meaning (p. 30).' This masterly work provides in effect a comprehensive prologue to social theory. It offers a link between seemingly opposed 'hard', 'positivist' ideas on the one hand, and 'soft', 'phenomenological', 'interactionist' ones on the other, and as such, will be used as a basic point of reference at many points in the subsequent text.

[6] *Exploration in Management*, Chapter 2. *See also* Jaques (1976), *A General Theory of Bureaucracy*, Chapter 2.

In trying to relate such terminology to that we have just established, one obvious interpretation is that 'formal' simply means 'manifest', that is, an authoritative, publicly proclaimed, statement of the prevailing institutions. But what then does 'informal' mean? If we have accepted that manifest statements are not always what they seem, we are already in the land of uncertainty and relativity, and we can hardly assign 'informal' to the status of what simply 'is'. ('Is', we might then enquire, in whose eyes – this actor's, that actor's, or the observer's?) If, alternatively, 'informal' is equated with the personal networks that grow up between particular individuals in organized groups, in contrast to the general forms of role and relationship which hold regardless of change of individuals, we are not speaking of what is actually institutionalized at all, but of ephemeral social situations which ebb and flow within it (see discussion in previous chapter).

Moreover, the idea of 'informal organization' can carry yet a different interpretation again, springing as it does from early studies of workers on the factory shop-floor banding together to protect themselves against possible exploitation by their employers. This would relate to the difference between two distinct social systems: 'formal' referring to the prime employment system in such cases, and 'informal' to some more or less explicit association of employees for mutual protection and advancement in relation to the employer, which might itself be institutionalized to some considerable degree.[7]

## Fundamental Approaches in Social Science: 'Objective Study', 'Action' and 'Behavioural' Views

Given this complexity in the very nature or substance of social institutions, how then does one go about studying them scientifically?

According to the impression created by many of the leading textbooks on social research method, the only really scientific approach, even in applied research of the kind with which we are concerned here, is through what may be broadly categorized as 'objective study'. Many subsidiary choices are offered: there is the individual case-study, or the wide-scale survey, or the experiment. But each, after some preliminary analysis of problems or needs, is seen as establishing a true scientific basis only with something called 'gather-

---

[7] See further discussion of the topic of so-called 'formal' and 'informal' organization in Brown (1965), 'Informal Organizations?' and Newman and Rowbottom (1968), *Organization Analysis*, Chapter 7.

ing the data'. Here, a variety of detailed methods present themselves: there is direct observation, interview, the use of questionnaires or even the study of existing written material and other secondary sources. Whichever is used, however, it is in the end always the researcher who decides what data he is going to collect, what counts as valid and significant, and what does not.[8]

Such approaches might be generally categorized as 'objective' on two scores. First, there is a tendency to assume that only 'hard facts' count, and better still facts in numerical form. This is regardless of how far the real situation actually offers hard facts, let alone quantitative measures, of any significance. Secondly, there is a tendency to see humans involved as objects to be cooly studied, assessed and measured, rather than as subjects whose values and actions continually alter and redefine the social reality under consideration.

At this point it is necessary to step back in order to consider two radically different views of man and the social world which may inform either research or intervention processes of various kinds. We shall distinguish these as 'action' approaches and 'behavioural' approaches.

In an 'action' approach, as its name implies, man is seen essentially as an actor; that is, as a being imbued with aims, purposes and the possibility of choice. The actor's own definition of the meaning of any situation is seen as a central and unavoidable fact in any work that is to be done – which is not to say, however, that the student or agent of change may not be allowed his own definitions of the situation as well. In 'behavioural' approaches by contrast, it is only the observer's or interventionist's view of the meaning of the situation which is allowed validity. Any activity or statement on the part of the 'subject' is seen as so much 'behaviour', the true cause and significance of which is to be determined by the observer, regardless of whether his view coincides with the subject's own interpretation

[8] This is certainly the predominant impression to be gathered from such established texts on social research method as those of Goode and Hatt (1953), *Methods in Social Research*; Festinger and Katz (1953), *Research Methods in the Behavioural Science*; Selltiz *et al.* (1965), *Research Methods in Social Relations*; Stacey (1969), *Methods of Social Research*; Galtung (1967), *Theory and Methods of Social Research* or Blalock (1970), *An Introduction to Social Research*. Festinger and Katz, for example, state: 'All scientists have as an ideal the objectification of their methods and techniques. That is, they aspire to observe, record and interpret events in such a fashion that independent observers can verify their findings.' Galtung uncompromisingly divides his book into two parts 'Data Collection' and 'Data Analysis'. Stacey follows the question 'how to start . . .' with the answer 'collection of primary data' etc. etc.

of the matter, were this latter indeed allowed as having any significance.

This distinction, or something like it, has of course been at the
heart of a running controversy about the nature of social science for
the last century or so. In broad terms it has divided those variously
described as 'positivist', 'tough-minded' or 'naturalistic' in outlook
from those usually described as 'tender-minded' or 'humanist'. In
the field of psychology it has divided the 'humanistic' or 'existentialist' psychologists from the 'behaviourists'. In sociology it has
divided the 'phenomenologists' (who have drawn on prominent
elements of Weber's work), the 'symbolic interactionists' and the
'ethnomethodologists' from the mainstream of the empiricists (who
draw their prime inspiration from Durkheim). The battle ranges too
in present-day political studies[9] and even intrudes into history.[10]
Indeed it, or something like it, stretches back at least to the beginnings of the modern period of history, with the growing threat of the
new empirical, scientific, outlook to established classical, humanist,
ideas.[11]

We have suggested that the present dominant theory of social
research method is one of 'objective study'. To a large extent the
leading advocates and practitioners, particularly those involved in
large-scale survey or experimental work could be identified with a
'behavioural' approach, as it has just been described (although, as
we shall see below, the carrying out of large-scale surveys is not in
principle inconsistent with an 'action' approach). At the same time
there is a significant and growing body of field researchers and

[9] See, for example, Easton's description of the latter-day revolt against 'behaviour-
ism' in political science (Easton, 1971, The Political System, Epilogue).

[10] See Carr (1961), What is History? Chapter 6.

[11] This topic in some form or other is discussed in practically every text on
method or philosophy of social sciences. See, for example, Ryan (1970), The
Philosophy of the Social Sciences, and Runciman (1971), Social Science and Political
Theory, Chapter 1. A classic modern statement of what is here called the 'action'
viewpoint is provided by Winch in The Idea of a Social Science (1958). Naturally,
statements of the precise nature of the dichotomy themselves vary. Some of the
closest to the view adopted here are provided by Thomas Szasz in Ideology and
Insanity (1974). Addressing himself to this problem from the standpoint of psychiatry
he distinguishes 'biological man' and 'social man' (p. 67) and two corresponding
and radically different attitudes to personal conduct: 'First, human behaviour may
be regarded as an event, essentially similar to other, non-human event . . . Second,
human behaviour may be regarded as a unique achievement, of which only man is
capable. Personal conduct is based on free choices of a sign-using, rule-following
and game-playing person whose action (author's italics) is often largely governed by
his future goals rather than by his past experiences (p. 199).'

writers on research methodology[12] who would certainly identify
themselves much more strongly with 'action' assumptions, as described above. Much social anthropology as well as sociological
research based on specific symbolic interactionist or ethnomethodological ideas, could be said to take an 'action' rather than a
'behavioural' standpoint. However, this research as a whole might
still in certain crucial respects be described as 'objective study', just
as much as most survey or experimental work. Gone is the obsessive
concern with numerical facts at all costs. Still remaining is the
detachment, even in so-called 'participative observation', from the
real concern and problems of the actors under view. Essentially the
aim is not to help the people immediately concerned to reshape their
own social world in a better form. The aim is more diffuse: to help
generate a deeper insight, greater 'verstehen', of the multitudinous
ways in which men in different cultures and subcultures view,
negotiate, construct and reconstruct the basic shapes of their own
social worlds. The basic concern is to understand the world as objectively as may be, but not to change it.

In neither such 'verstehen' research then, nor in most survey or
experimental work is there an inbuilt concern to help in the immediate situation under study, whatever may be the concern to
contribute to more indirect or long-term social change.

Because of this, certain rather formidable problems arise. First,
there is the problem of access. What is to persuade the would-be
subject to collaborate in the research, and to devote time and energy
to providing the necessary answers or information? Then, there is the
problem of commitment. Even if the subjects do amiably agree to
submit to the demands of the researcher's relentless curiosity, how
can one be sure that any information offered is a true image of the
underlying reality, or is even offered in good faith? Again, there is the
well-known interaction, or contamination, effect. How can subjects
be prevented from responding consciously or unconsciously to the interests of the researcher; how can they be stopped from tending to give
the sort of answers which they feel will be approved of; how indeed
can one prevent their actual perceptions of social reality from shifting
a little according to the very way in which questions are framed?[13]

[12] See Cicourel (1964), Method and Measurement in Sociology; Bruyn (1966), The
Human Perspective in Sociology; Denzin (1970), The Research Act in Sociology; Becker
(1970), Sociological Work: Method and Substance.
[13] Many of these problems are discussed in the texts on research method referred
to above, which are based on social interactionist or phenomenological assumptions.
See also Rosenthal (1966), Experimenter Effects in Behavioural Research, and Friedman
(1967), The Social Nature of Psychological Research.

## Collaborative Exploration

In social analysis an 'action' approach is inevitably adopted. The very idea of 'social institutions' is an 'action' one and has no significance in a behavioural view of man. Moreover, social analysis is firmly wedded to the idea of helping those with problems in particular situations. And wherever people spontaneously raise problems which concern proper forms of social institutions, it may be taken as axiomatic that uncertainty and controversy about existing forms will prevail. If the actors themselves are fundamentally unsure about the existing form of the material under consideration (in this case the social institutions within which they act); if questions of existence are inextricably interwoven with issues of value or desirability; and if all these are experienced as problems pressing for relief or solution by those caught up in them; then there is only one thing to be done. The researcher must abandon any pretence of 'objective study'. He must take off his jacket so to speak, and join with those same actors in the difficult job of analysing, clarifying, identifying alternatives and predicting consequences. He must abandon the role of the independent observer and become to some degree a participant. He must be concerned not just with facts, but with values and choices. In short, he must join in what can best be described as 'collaborative exploration'.

However, in adopting such an approach the researcher has to observe certain conditions, to pay a certain price that is, if he is to pursue it successfully:

  (1) he can only work where the actors concerned are themselves willing to work (not just to allow themselves to be 'studied'); that is by definition only where there are felt problems of pressing concern;
  (2) he has necessarily to forego, therefore, the possibility of any systematic pre-planning of the ground to be covered, the subjects to be comprehensively explored, or of the 'data' to be gathered;
  (3) he has to accept the confidentiality of what he hears and discusses until such time as clearance for wider publication is specifically agreed, and has indeed to accept the possibility that clearance for some material may never be gained.

At the same time some of the considerable problems identified above as implicit in objective studies are avoided or minimized. To start with, given collaborative exploration under these conditions, the problem of access is considerably diminished. For as may be imagined, any offer to study actors' problems as they themselves define them and with whatever priority they give them, which is linked also to strong reassurances on control of confidentiality, is likely to seem more attractive than one framed simply in terms of the researcher's needs and interests. Again, it follows that the commitment of the person concerned to get at the truth of what really holds in practice is considerably enhanced where he sees himself an active partner in a collaboration addressed to his own problems, rather than as a passive research 'subject'. And finally, in collaborative exploration the so-called contamination effect is dealt with (almost paradoxically) by incorporating it explicitly into the main scheme of the approach, rather than by attempting to minimise or circumvent it in some way. The researcher no longer strives to avoid the influence of his own ideas and approaches on the subject. Indeed, he positively seeks to influence and affect those he is working with. (The corrective to subjectivity, as we shall see later, is not any futile attempt to avoid all influence or to attain perfect objectivity, but rather in the testing of prediction through experience.) In any concern to get to a social science which is committed, relevant and reality-based, the importance of these advantages can hardly be over-emphasized.

## General Scope of Collaborative Exploration

It has been said that where the actual subject matter of social research is one the very nature of which is uncertain or contentious in the eyes of those involved in it, and where this is combined with a concern to help those involved to improve the situation, collaborative exploration is called for rather than what might be broadly characterized as 'objective study'. Immediate help with problems about social institutions – social analysis – falls readily into this category. However, the possibility of, or indeed the need for, collaborative exploration is not limited to the study of social institutions.

Surveying the general scheme, it may be supposed that collaborative exploration is called for wherever research is undertaken which aims to be of immediate help in problems which are conceived in 'action' terms. This implies that the people who express the problems are seen as quite capable (with help) of making up their own minds about what actions to take to alleviate their problems, and (after due consideration) about what objectives, constraints and standards to set for themselves. This would contrast with situations

where the people concerned, by reason of incapacity or ignorance –
say because of extreme youth or extreme age – were not able to
understand in any useful way the matters at issue, or to decide and
undertake for themselves the ameliorative action called for.[14]

Thus, there is obvious scope for employment of collaborative exploration in certain kinds of psychotherapeutic work with either
individuals or groups. There is obvious scope too for its use in two
further aspects of organized activity identified in the previous chapter – (collective) programmes and (collective) technologies. In 'operational research' for example (an activity conceived here as coming
within the programming field), there is every reason to think that an
approach of collaborative exploration would be in every way more
fitting and more successful than one in which the expert operational
researcher 'studies' the situation at length and finally emerges with
his unilaterally conceived 'recommendations'. The same applies no
doubt where, say, outside advisers are employed in developing coun-
tries to help local communities to use improved technologies of various kinds; or where expert consulting engineers are called in to help
in technical problems in large industrial concerns.

### The Place of Systematic Fact-Finding in Collaborative Exploration in General, and Social Analysis in Particular

These last illustrations raise an important general point about collaborative exploration. Although we have sharply contrasted it with
'objective study' which places heavy emphasis on systematic fact-
finding, there is no need to assume that systematic fact-finding never
has any proper place in collaborative exploration. Neither the idea
of collaborative analysis, nor the 'action' view-point from which it
stems denies for a moment the possibility that many aspects of the
social, let alone the physical, situation of actors may be taken as
having unequivocal 'factual' status.[15] Nor does it deny the possibility
that clear knowledge of such facts, where they exist, may be of help

[14] In so-called 'clinical research' in medicine, knowledge is gradually built up
from cases of individual patients spontaneously presenting themselves for treatment
one by one, rather than by pre-designed experiment. This provides an example of a
kind of research which is oriented to immediate help. Nevertheless, it does not
involve full 'collaborative exploration'. The prevailing assumption is that the doctor's understanding of the issues concerned greatly surpasses that of his 'patient' – a
'behavioural' rather than an 'action' view.

[15] It might be useful here to have regard to the distinction made by Stephen
Pepper between the rough evidence, or 'facts' of commonsense perception – what he

in problem-solving. In programming work, for example, it would be strange indeed if the exploration did not reveal at many points the need for the systematic collection of data on actual costs, demands, delays, clients dealt with, completions and the like. And in many kinds of technical development too, there are obvious aspects where factual or quantitative information can aid assessment or decision.

In the specific field of development of social institutions, however – the field with which social analysis happens to be concerned – it appears to be the case that there is usually little by way of systematic collection of facts that is of much help. For one thing, although social institutions will often present facets or characteristics which can be regarded as matters of unequivocal fact (as has been noted), it is usually the case that such features are not of the kind that is of great significance in institutional design or change. Thus, for example, it may often be possible to produce reliable statistics of the number of posts of a given grade, or the number of operational units, factories, hospitals, offices and so on which exist in some large undertaking. But attempts to produce factual information about more fundamental matters such as, say, the number of managerial levels which exist, the functions undertaken by particular divisions, the content of duties and authority attaching to particular posts, often leave huge doubts as to the significance of the results obtained.[16]

Elliott Jaques has suggested that in the 'time-span of discretion' a reliable instrument has been discovered for producing factual information about the level of responsibility in various organizational posts. But even here, it is readily agreed that no useful data can be obtained in principle where there is significant doubt or confusion about the exact content of work expected in any post – which is again, so often exactly what is found in problem situations.[17]

---

refers to as 'dubitanda' – and the refined evidence of observations which can be repeated and corroborated by many observers – what he refers to precisely as 'data' (Pepper, 1942, *World Hypothesis – A Study in Evidence*). It is this second, and special, kind of 'fact' which we are now considering.

[16] This is a general criticism of what was described in the previous chapter as the recent wave of 'textural' studies of organization, starting with Joan Woodward's large-scale survey of firms in Essex (Woodward, 1965, *Industrial Organization: Theory and Practice*). This and the many survey studies which followed could be argued to have assumed far too readily that there are abundant 'facts' about fundamental organizational variables, which are just waiting for the picking, so to speak.

[17] 'If a manager . . . is unable to make a firm decision about target completion times and quality standard limits, then you cannot carry out time-span measurement. The necessary data do not exist. It is as though you were trying to measure the length of an irregular wad of cotton wool' (Jaques, 1964, *Time-Span Handbook*, p. 28).

So much for usual non-availability of clear-cut facts about prevailing social institutions themselves; or at least, facts of any great significance. Added to this it is usually difficult to discover any other associated facts or statistics, which have any direct relevance to decisions about the best design for social institutions, or for that matter, direct relevance to decisions after the event about the value of any actual institutional changes made. (This last point is explored in greater depth in Chapter 9.) Exact statistics of strikes and stoppages, for example, do not in themselves contribute to the design of better industrial relations procedures – though the high incidence of such things may be exactly what causes attention to turn to the matter. Staff turnover figures do not help in themselves to design better appeals procedures, or staff development systems. Statistics on output or profit, or patients seen and discharged, do not help to design industrial undertakings or hospitals.

However, there are occasions, if rare, when factual surveys can make a genuine contribution to social-analytic exploration. In addition to the systematic collection of 'time-span of discretion' data in the Glacier Project and its correlation with 'felt fair pay' data, a need was also established at an early point to undertake the systematic collection of 'earning progression' data of numbers of employees, in connection with the development of salary and wage review procedures.[18] In both these cases it was agreed by all the actors concerned that the systematic gathering of factual information on these particular matters might well prove a useful step in the search for greater insight into the problems facing them.

## The Dangers of Overriding Concern with Systematic Surveys

There is then no clash in principle between collaborative exploration and systematic fact-finding exercises, even in connection with the development of social institutions. However, whatever the surface similarities at particular points of time between systematic surveys undertaken within a collaborative–exploratory approach and an 'objective study' approach, there will be very different underlying assumptions at work.

[18] *See* Jaques (1956), *Measurement of Responsibility* and Jaques (1967), *Equitable Payment*. John Evans has described some of the problems that arise where it is attempted to undertake systematic surveys of time-span of discretion *outside* a social-analytic, that is a problem-oriented, framework (Evans, 1971, 'Contrasting Task Analysis Procedures in Consultancy-Based and Survey-Based Research').

In collaborative exploration, systematic fact collection will always be secondary. The primary concern will always be with helping the actor or actors concerned to articulate their own problems, needs and possible solutions. If facts on certain matters truly do help, then they can be got; but the independent agent concerned in collaborative exploration must never be seduced into thinking that data collection and statistical analysis represent the quintessential elements of a scientific approach. Moreover, if the facts really are all that relevant to the problem in hand, and the actors concerned see this as forcibly as the researchers, then it is quite likely that the actors themselves will be more than willing to collect these facts themselves (assuming indeed that they are not already available, given their obvious relevance).

Where the researcher finds himself personally involved in extensive data collection or survey work, it is always perhaps time to pause and consider just how consistent this is with genuine collaborative exploration. The doubt will be raised even more strongly should the researcher ever find himself in a situation where he is trying to get information from respondents who do not see what his questions are driving at, or what relevance they have to their own immediate problems.

The idea of collaboration is one that is frequently stressed in the literature on 'action research' and 'organization development'.[19] However, it is striking how much reference there is in this same broad body of literature to 'data collection', frequently in the form of attitude surveys which are at a later point fed back to those who have been surveyed.[20] Admittedly, it has been suggested on occasion that those who are to be surveyed should be involved in preliminary discussion of the kind of data to be collected,[21] or even that organizational members should completely design and undertake their own surveys.[22] Often however, the ambivalance about genuine collaboration with all the actors involved (and not just some of the more powerful or senior who are sponsoring or financing the work) is only too apparent.

Collaboration must surely always imply an 'action' framework.

[19] See for example, Schein (1969), *Process Consultation: Its Role in Organizational Development*; Bennis, Benne and Chin (1970), *The Planning of Change*; Rapoport (1970), 'Three Dilemmas in Action Research'.

[20] See, for example, Mann (1957), *Studying and Creating Change*; Bennis (1969), *Organization Development*; Lawrence and Lorsch (1969), *Developing Organizations*; Schein (1969), op. cit.

[21] Miles et al. (1970), *The Consequence of Survey Feedback: Theory and Evaluation*.

[22] Revans (1976), *Action Learning in Hospitals*.

Wherever heavy emphasis is placed on the establishment of objective data according to the researcher's own definition, wherever overt reference is made to 'diagnosis', wherever explicit prescriptions are laid down by the researcher as to what constitutes a 'good' organization,[23] the underlying assumption is clearly a behavioural one rather than an action one, as we have just distinguished them. In some of the famous 'experiments' in organizational change[24] we are light-years away from any genuine idea of collaboration in which the actors concerned (in this case, shop-floor workers) pose their own goals and problems, as well as joining fully in the exploration of the 'facts'.

Here, we come close indeed to the point where intervention becomes manipulation, and where so-called social science becomes an instrument for imposing the aims and ideologies of one group on others less powerful and less articulate.

[23] Lawrence and Lorsch (1969), op. cit., and Blake and Mouton (1969), *Building a Dynamic Corporation Through Grid Organization Development*, provide prime examples of what we would describe here as prescriptive approaches to organizational development.

[24] Coch and French (1948), *Overcoming Resistance to Change*; Morse and Reimer (1956), *The Experimental Change of a Major Organizational Variable*.

# PART II

# What Happens in Practice

# 5  Teasing out Formulations

We have now established the general field with which social analysis is concerned: enactable change in social institutions. We have also established the general nature of the approach, which has been described as one of 'collaborative exploration'.

In Part II we turn to what actually happens in practice. We shall consider the actual procedure adopted in project work. We shall consider the continual attempt to refine the language of everyday organizational life, and to clarify the various concepts which it embodies, and how these contribute to the scientific character of the endeavour. For a start we consider in this chapter the central activity of the social-analytic process, which is one of 'teasing out' from the rich mixture of problems, needs, conflicting perceptions and beliefs in real-life situations, formulations of the kinds of social institutions that appear to be called for; that is, what is requisite. We shall consider too, some of the difficulties and dilemmas that are likely to be encountered in attempting to do this.

## The Process of 'Teasing out' Requisite Formulations

Let us suppose that the social analyst has actually become engaged in helping members of an organized body to explore some problems which, as far as can be judged, centre on inadequate or ill-defined institutions. (The exact steps by which such involvement is engineered will be discussed in the next chapter but one.) As was seen in the previous chapter, the very act of description of social institutions is a problematic matter. Sometimes one can talk straightforwardly about institutions or particular aspects of them as they factually and unequivocally exist. More usually, and particularly where there are suspected problems about them, it is necessary to abandon any straightforward search for what 'is'. Account has to be taken of the possibility of three different kinds of statements. First, as we have seen, there are statements of the 'manifest' situation (statements of prevailing social institutions as displayed in authoritative enactments). Then there are statements of the 'assumed' situation (any statements by the people concerned of the views they actually act upon at any time). Finally, there are statements about what is 'requisite' (statements which argue for the adoption of particular forms of social institutions to meet given needs or requirements, regardless of what may be manifest, or even assumed, for the moment).

In the course of exploration, statements of these three kinds will tend to follow a certain sequence. Thus discussion may start with a reference to any manifest statements (official reports, charts, memoranda, job descriptions and the like) which may exist. This may lead to discussion about participants' own assumptions about how things 'really' operate. And this in turn may lead to further discussion about how things could be clarified or improved; that is, to what is requisite. (Indeed, the cycle could be extended further. Given general sanction for emerging ideas of requisite institutions, any authoritative enactments or statements which are made thereafter then become the new 'manifest' situation. And then as time passes, the emergence of new conditions or requirements may create new shifts in practice, so that once again gaps start to show between people's assumptions and the once appropriate, officially promulgated system. And so on.)

There is, however, an even deeper significance in this sequence. It is only by careful removal of the outer layers as it were, by steady progression from the surface statements through the deeper assumptions, more or less consciously made, that one can hope to penetrate to the inner core of understanding what the realities of the situation are actually demanding.

Indeed, although three discrete and logically distinct stages are described here, exploration of any particular problem situation has much more the feel in practice of a continuous process. People do not usually have perceptions of their social situations precisely formulated and ready to retail on demand. Clear statements have to be prompted by such questions as 'what would you tend to do if or when such-and-such a situation arose?' or 'how would you be expected to react if so-and-so acted thus?' In other words, it is only by carefully examining people's typical behaviour or by testing with them what their behaviour would be likely to be in certain critical situations, that the existing assumptions on which they work can be brought out into the daylight for review. And, in the course of this, the shift from what 'is' to what 'ought to be' is both inevitable and imperceptible.

In consequence of this last point, written reports produced for the participants in social-analytic project work rarely if ever record separate and distinct statements of 'assumed' and 'requisite' views of the nature of the social institutions concerned. Sometimes, quotations from official statements will be included to register what manifestly prevails. Often there is considerable reference to the starting situation in terms of circumstantial facts, problems, concerns and the like. But actual analysis, once embarked upon, is usually driven straight through to various statements of what is considered requisite.

Underlying this whole process is what might appear perhaps to be a somewhat optimistic belief – but one nevertheless confirmed by experience. This is a belief that in moving away from official statements and creating new assumptions about appropriate behaviour, people are already consciously or unconsciously moving to what in prevailing conditions, makes more sense and helps to solve their problems.[1]

At the centre of social-analytic work in practice then is this 'teasing out' process – the careful feeling around, the removal of the surface knots and tangles, and the gradual exposure of the underlying forms. However, it is also part of the essential character of the work that the analyst is not just interested in helping people to move forward by feel or intuition. He is intent on understanding and exposing the principles which govern the choice or outcome at each stage of development. He is looking for explicit *formulations* of the sorts of social institutions that are requisite, given certain constraints and requirements.

## An Example of 'Teasing out' of Formulations

Let us consider an actual example that illustrates these various levels of perception of social institutions, and the process of the 'teasing out' of alternative formulations or models of the requisite.[2]

[1] This idea of the requisite, already imminent as it were, in actual working practice is clearly expressed by Elliott Jaques in 'Social Analysis and the Glacier Project' (Jaques, 1965c). He has often in discussion used the phrase 'teasing out' with reference to the process of getting to the requisite.

[2] An initial discussion of the particular problem to be considered was offered in *Social Services Departments* (pp. 119–21).

It is common in Social Services Departments in local authorities to provide the teams of social workers who are situated in specific 'area' offices, with support in the form of a small group of administrative and clerical staff who work closely alongside them. Experience suggests that there nearly always follows a problem of the organizational relationship of these administrative staff, on the one hand to the chief social worker with the team – the Area Officer, and on the other hand to senior administrative staff within the central headquarters organization (Figure 5.1). The administrative staff

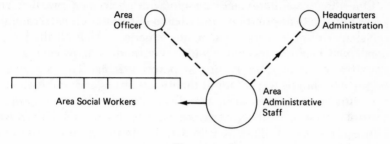

*Figure 5.1*

concerned are pulled in two directions. On the one hand they feel part of the total area team, and to this extent, under the influence of the Area Officer. On the other hand they are clerks and administrators, not professional social workers, and much of their work is closely linked to the headquarters administrative division within the Department, headed by the chief administrator who is typically not a professional social worker.

Manifest statements of organization vary. Some show the clerical staff simply as part of the main administrative division, and leave it at that. Others show them as 'under' the Area Officer with perhaps a 'dotted line' to Headquarters Administration.

Such situations have been explored in a number of social-analytic projects. Discussions with various of the parties involved about the way they actually behave in practice, and the assumptions implicit in this behaviour, usually reveal some degree of dissatisfaction or unease with manifest statements as they stand. 'They are supposed to be part of the Chief Administrator's staff, but they really work for me of course' (Area Officer). 'I know the Area Officers are trying to take them over, but I shall resist it strongly. It won't work' (Chief Administrator). Probing unearths further interesting material: 'I should certainly want Administration to recruit them – and to replace them if they were off sick for any length of time.' 'If we had a bad one, after I had done all I could to rectify the situation, I would turn the problem over to the Chief Administrator.' 'I haven't time to be concerned with their *technical* training' (statements by the Area Officer). 'Of course I don't expect to control their work day by day.' 'Well, yes, I would be bound to get the Area Officer's views on any question of their competence or potential.' 'It is really up to me to encourage them to apply for higher grade jobs, if they're suitable. Some of the married women never think of applying otherwise' (all statements by the Chief Administrator).

One digs, questions, faces people with their own practice and poses hypothetical situations, in order to test assumptions. Gradually the shapes of an interesting structure emerge, which all the parties concerned begin to recognize with relief (and perhaps even a little embarrassment at their failure to perceive it earlier) as one that might well indeed work. Out of the uncertainties and ambiguities of the initial scene comes an image of the requisite situation in which control, and responsibility therefore, is to be shared in a defined way between the Area Officer and the Chief Administrator. It is a situation which, as it happens, had been identified in earlier years within the Glacier Project, under the name 'co-management'.[3] Its general nature can be stated formally as follows:

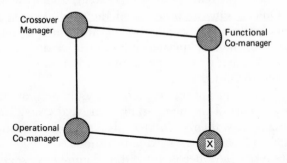

Co-management arises where it is desired to *manage* the work of X in technical, occupational or professional respects, in conjunction with that

[3] 'Co-management' was used at one period of social-analytic work as synonymous with 'attachment' and indeed the second term is generally used for preference in both *Hospital Organization* and *Social Services Departments*. However, later developments in thinking have suggested that the term 'attachment' is more fruitfully applied to a wider variety of organizational situations of which co-management is but one particular kind. In the instance described above, it is essentially the conception of co-management that is under consideration.

of other practitioners in the same function or field, whilst leaving intact a clear line of operational accountability. This is achieved by X's functional manager attaching him to the staff of some operational manager.

The arrangement relies on the existence of a 'crossover' manager who can set or approve policies which are binding on both co-managers, and who can adjudicate on any unresolved issue which divides them.

Specifically, the functional co-manager is accountable in respect of X:
– for helping to select him according to professional criteria, and for inducting him in matters relating to the field concerned;
– for helping him to deal with technical problems in the field concerned;
– for co-ordinating his work with that of other similar practitioners in the field;
– for keeping himself informed about X's work, for discussing possible improvements in standards with him and for reporting to the operational co-manager any sustained or significant deficiencies or lapses from established policy in X's work;
– for appraising his technical competence;
– for providing for his technical training.

The operational co-manager is accountable in respect of X:
– for helping to select him and for inducting him in operational matters;
– for assigning work to him and for allocating resources;
– for appraising his general performance and ability.

Both co-managers have right of veto on appointment, right to provide official appraisals, and right to decide if X is unsuitable for performing any of the work for which they are accountable.

The functional co-manager can give instructions provided that:
– they are given within policies established by the 'crossover' manager, binding on both co-managers;
– they do not conflict with policies or operating instructions issued by the operational co-manager.

Since the functional co-manager is accountable for X's functional competence, he must have the authority to monitor the operational co-manager with respect to policy in the functional area, to ensure that X's competence is being utilized in a professionally appropriate way.[4]

However, the analyst does not leave it at this. In order to emphasize the situation of choice open to actors with whom he is collaborating, he searches for further alternatives. Two readily come to mind. In the first, the area administrative staff are in fact fully managed by the Area Officer. But this implies for example that the latter is responsible for their career progression and training – on any adequate definition of 'management' that is. In this case Headquarters Administration would have a rather more restricted role. They might have responsibility for recruitment of clerical staff

---

[4] *See Social Services Departments*, p. 249.

perhaps, and also for co-ordinating the development of, and monitoring subsequent adherence to, standard clerical procedures. Alternatively the staff could be fully managed by the Chief Administrator, and simply 'outposted' by him to Area Offices where they could be thought of as in a relationship to social workers, of simply providing services on request. One implication of this second alternative model is that the Area Officer could not himself lay down general policies or procedures binding on clerical staff, in contrast to asking specific and discrete services of them. Moreover he would have no right to comment on their individual suitability for appointment, or on the adequacy of their individual performances thereafter.

Which of these three possibilities is best? From many points of view it seems that the first one – the co-management model – makes the best sense. But ultimately, it is up to the actors concerned to make the judgements. Apart from the general consequences identified, they will also have to take account of special and local circumstances. It is possible, for example, that there is a highly capable Chief Administrator in the situation, or perhaps, on the other hand, he himself is only barely adequate; perhaps the Area Officers are already grossly overburdened; and so on. In the end it is not the analyst's job to choose, but simply to help uncover the possibilities and their general implications and consequences.

## The Elucidatory Role of the Social Analyst

As this example illustrates, the social analyst's role is not a prescriptive one, but one which may more aptly be described as 'elucidatory'. It is within the role of the analyst to stimulate exploratory activity, to collect impressions and views, to analyse existing situations and problems and even to proffer alternative reconstructions. It is not within his role to say what should then be done in the particular case or to suggest it or insinuate it in any way. This is a real distinction: analysis and illumination are not simply disguised forms of advice or recommendation. As Elliott Jaques put it in summarizing his own experience at Glacier Metal:

> It might be said that the analyst in fact makes recommendations in the content of his analytical comments and reports. In a limited sense, I suppose that is true. But they are recommendations only in the sense of being statements to the effect that 'I think that the following factors are likely to be significant in resolving your difficulty'; or 'Taking what you have said, and putting it together with your own organizational policy,

the following type of organization would result'; or 'It seems to me that there is an inconsistency between the steps you are proposing and your previous decisions on this matter'; or 'I think you are trying to deny the findings from our previous analyses'.

Each of these statements is a recommendation to pay attention to something, or to consider a given possibility, or an inconsistency, or a new finding. They are definitely not recommendations to the effect that 'I think you should do so-and-so. I believe the Company would be better off if you did'; or 'Your Mr A is not good enough for the post he is in. You ought to transfer him to this other role'; or 'I would urge you to change your policy in the following manner'.[5]

The social analyst offers formulations, not solutions. Solutions are total answers to any problem situation. As such their determination must necessarily rest with the actors intimately involved in that particular situation, since the best total response must include judgements about the significance and importance of a host of specific circumstances that the analyst is in no position to make. What the analyst can offer is at once more partial, and more general. It is his job to point to certain general features and the relationships between them. Taking due account of the particular circumstances in which his collaborators find themselves, he is saying in effect 'here is one general way of construing the situation, and these are its characteristics' or 'here is a possible general line of action, and these are its general consequences'.

In order that his formulations are not simply mistaken for proposed solutions, it is very important for the analyst to offer not just one, but two or more alternative formulations of what may be requisite wherever possible (as described in the case-study just discussed) even where there is a strong feeling perhaps that one of them is going to be much more relevant than the rest. One reason for doing this is because it reassures the actor that the choice does after all lie in his hands. The analyst is not simply moving into some covert prescriptive role. So long as each of the possibilities described has some degree of credibility it does not hurt the actor to be presented with a number of options. He is rapidly able to discard those formulations that are not serviceable for him – with some additional confidence gained perhaps from the fact that he has not simply opted for the first possibility to come to mind.

Over and above this, experience has shown that the process of looking quite consciously for alternatives rather than just for single

[5] Jaques (1965c), p. 33.

formulations, often does reveal or suggest further possibilities of unexpected merit or interest. At the very least it often throws new light on an obvious 'best' model, or allows a better formulation of it than had been conceived before the broader search was undertaken.

Making it clear that he is not trying to judge the merits of alternative possibilities, or the comparative strengths of various specific and local factors which point to one rather than the other, enormously strengthens the analyst's ability to get to the heart of the general problems at issue. As Jaques says again:

> The social-analytic relationship is one in which the interviewee has nothing to lose, and has nothing to gain but a better and more explicit understanding of his own views and experience – an understanding which, when put together with a clarification of the views of other members involved in a project, may lead to a conceptually novel solution to a problem. Under such conditions, my experience has consistently been that individuals produce a constructive digest of their own experience, which contains elements or sometimes whole features of the principles and concepts for which it is the social-analyst's responsibility to listen.[6]

By opting firmly for an elucidatory role the social analyst avoids two opposing dangers implicit in the prescriptive approach, often adopted, for example, by many management consultants or 'management services' staff. On the one hand there is the danger of summary rejection by members of the organization concerned; on the other there is the danger of complete assimilation. Thus, in the one situation the consultant, after some intensive but short-lived exploration makes explicit 'recommendations'. However he does not really understand the situation; he is not soaked in it; he has not lived with the problem concerned and he is not going to have to live with the solution proposed. Intuitively, those involved will find many or all of the proposals unacceptable, even if they are perhaps unable to put all their objections into words. In consequence, the recommendations are formally rejected, or laid to one side: the project has failed. In the other and contrasted situation the consultant (here regarded as highly 'successful') stays with his clientele through the period of change, and indeed helps to implement it. As change proceeds, the crudity or inadequacy of his initial recommendations may well become apparent and, if so, modifications are quietly made. The system becomes dependent upon him, and he becomes captured by the system. He is no longer an independent

[6] Jaques (1965c), p. 44.

professional agent of change. He has become an active member of the social group concerned.

By combining a process of collaborative exploration with a strictly elucidatory role then, the social analyst preserves a fine and precious balance. On the one hand he becomes deeply involved in, and thus manifests his personal concern with, immediate and pressing problems of organized social life. On the other, by sticking to the elucidation of general principles and by avoiding being drawn into the personal and the particular, he retains his independence and his scientific objectivity.

## How Much Initiative?

This last discussion leads naturally to the related one of how much initiative it is legitimate for the analyst to take. The dangers at either extreme are readily identifiable.

If the analyst shows too little initiative then nothing very much happens, and nothing very much is achieved. Problems are aired, attitudes are exposed, views are exchanged and finally the dust settles, leaving the scene much as it was before. At the extreme, the analyst has simply acted as a recorder of views, as a mirror for problems. If, on the other hand, the analyst shows too much initiative, then conscious of it or not, he assumes in fact a prescriptive role. His own views of how the problem should be tackled start to dominate the scene. Here, he says, are the possibilities, but of course (he adds) you might be wise to pay good regard to *this* one.

The problem becomes particularly acute in regard to initiative in introducing new conceptions and new terminology; for here is a field in which the analyst must make a distinctive contribution to the collaborative work. How far should the analyst be ready to introduce general conceptions which have already been developed in previous work when he sees, or thinks he sees, a situation in which they may be relevant again? How far should he introduce already worked-out models of role-relationships such as the 'co-management' one just described; or 'managerial', 'supervisory', 'co-ordinating', 'service-giving' models and the like; or other specific conceptions which have been evolved on such topics as discrete levels of work, or particular dimensions of professional practice which affect organizations?

If he pushes too much or too fast, sooner or later there is an inevitable reaction. At first people start to make remarks half-jokingly, half-nervously about the special terms or categories employed: 'have I got it right?', 'what do you call it again?', 'what is the Brunel answer to this?' Soon they begin to dissociate themselves from the real collaborative work, whilst still perhaps retaining on the surface a friendly relationship. Two sets of papers start to circulate. First there are project reports drafted by the analyst in the 'official' project language. Then there are the everyday executive memoranda couched in homely (if inexact) language, in which the real work is transacted and on which actual decisions are based.

In this dilemma the analyst must hold firm to one golden principle: this is *the principle of staying at all times with the actors.* Of course he must introduce new ideas, precise conceptions, detailed and explicit formulations. Indeed, he may stimulate, question, even on occasion bring up with a shock, those he is working with.[7] But how far he does so, and at what stage must always be guided by the particular person with whom he is collaborating and the particular social and cultural setting in which they are both working. It is no use preparing a note which is full of polysyllabic words and elaborate conceptions for some relatively unsophisticated collaborator, one who is not perhaps even accustomed to using the written word in his normal work. What is good for the research chemist or personnel director is not necessarily good for the shop foreman or laundry worker. Then again, length of involvement may be crucial. Ideas that need lengthy introduction at an early stage of discussion with a person may be capable of being expressed in a more compressed form at a later point.

## The Correctives to Biased or Inadequate Formulations

Given that the analyst is likely to take the initiative in posing explicit organizational formulations, there is another worry. Even if they are

[7] As Bennis, Benne and Chin point out, a genuine collaborative relationship does not eschew all conflict, and any that does so is likely to be a tepid and unproductive affair (Bennis, Benne and Chin, 1970, *The Planning of Change*, pp. 147–53). The problem of losing contact with the clientele is not of course peculiar to social analysis – *see* Rapoport (1970), 'Three Dilemmas in Action Research' for a general discussion of 'rejection phenomena' in action research; Clark (1972), 'Sanction – A Critical Element in Action Research' for a candid analysis of an action research project that failed; and Argyris (1973), *Intervention Theory and Method* for various case-studies of 'ineffective intervention'. *See also* Dale (1974), 'Coercive Persuasion and the Role of the Change Agent' for a general discussion of the wide variety of modes of work open to the change agent, ranging from outright direction at one extreme, through advice, analysis of specific problems, to general re-education at the other. As he points out, a prime question in choosing an appropriate strategy is just how much uncertainty and ambiguity the person who is being worked with can stand.

acceptable, how does he know they are right? True, they will be explored as fully as possible in discussions, but this is not to say that all the issues have even been identified, let alone correctly analysed. How can limitations in the analyst's own thinking be overcome? How can the evangelical impact of his own enthusiasms and preconceptions be prevented from colouring the whole proceedings? How can he avoid the insidious influence of a personal attraction to this particular individual and his particular ideas and concerns, or a spontaneous disinterest in relation to the other?

Of course, he can try as far as possible to adopt a 'professional' stance. He can consciously attempt to see problems in objective terms irrespective of personal likes and dislikes, to put service before self-interest, to make a point of offering the same quality of service to all, to make clear the limits to his sphere of competence and so on.[8]

In the end however, it must be recognized that none of the ideological and personal biases identified above can be completely removed. The analyst cannot by his own efforts change himself from what he is – an individual person with his own particular persuasions, theories and prejudices. Nor, experience shows, is the right formulation likely to be hit upon straightway in the first round of attack upon the problem. The great correctives to both these difficulties are time and test. It is of the essence of social analysis that formulations are not simply arrived at as once-and-for-all conclusions in some process of abstracted debate. They are produced as working hypotheses in a carefully engineered situation where all the incentives are to put them to the test of actual practice; then, if necessary, to revise and review them in the light of experience; then to move to further test; and so on. (The steps which may be taken to help achieve such a situation in practice are discussed in Chapter 7.) Indeed, what has to be accepted here has to be accepted for all scientific work. To practise science is not somehow to avoid completely all partiality or self-deception, but to put oneself in the position of being able to test for any bias or errors which these may cause.[9]

[8] We are consciously echoing here Talcott Parsons' analysis of the various value-bases of the professional role: 'affective neutrality', 'collectivity orientation', 'universality' and 'functional specificity' (Parsons, 1951, *The Social System*, pp. 434–5).

[9] This, of course, is broadly the Popperian view of science – *see* Popper (1966), *The Open Society and Its Enemies*, Chapter 23, and Popper (1974), *Conjectures and Refutations*, Chapter 1. The controversy between this and the opposing idea of science as inevitably developing from some or other ideological base is considered at length in Lakatos and Musgrave (1970), *Criticism and the Growth of Knowledge*. Dahrendorf, in the course of a comprehensive examination of the place of values in

## Problems of Warring Parties

Another problem sometimes facing the social analyst is that of war-
ring parties. By this is meant not just a situation where people differ
in opinion about how things ought generally to function, but also
one where there are entrenched battles about the proper extent of
the role, status or authority of those in existing positions, or even
long-standing conflicts of a more personal nature. Many projects
start exactly from a point where some such organizational conflict or
confusion is felt to exist, or from the point where the behaviour or
attitude of one person or party is felt by some other to be reaching an
intolerable level. How in such a situation does the social analyst
avoid being 'captured' by one or other party? How indeed does he
avoid exacerbating the conflict?

In the first place the social analyst must attempt to gain the
confidence of all parties, and here the importance of individual
discussions with all those prominently involved is vital (as will be
amplified in Chapter 7). Time and again a highly charged,
suspicious individual has been won over for the project when he has
had a chance to see for himself in private discussion that the analyst
is not concerned with working on personal judgements, is not trying
to support or engineer particular outcomes, and is simply trying to
establish some of the basic realities about which this particular
protagonist may have important perceptions to contribute.

In any group discussions which may follow, what does not help in
this situation however is a report from the analyst which merely sets
out the various viewpoints, or one which simply reproduces or col-
lates straightforward statements of the difficulties, in however imper-
sonal a way. The direct reporting back of problems or conflicting
attitudes without any further addition merely serves to enhance
anxiety. It is essential in this situation that the social analyst should
start to offer some positive analysis of the situation. He should
include, if possible, formulations of alternative models of action with
their various objective consequences (as far as these can be seen),
however unrealizable some of these formulations may appear to be
on the face of things. The aim here is to take the problem out of the

---

social sciences, argues the desirability of the scientist's moral commitment, in contrast to what ought to be the value-free nature of his science itself (Dahrendorf,
1968b, 'Values and Social Science'). In the end, the value-free nature of science
rests in the possibility of confronting theories, however arrived at, with facts; and it
is in this and this only that the ultimate safeguard of objectivity rests.

realm of personal attitude and emotional response, and into the realm of objective and reasoned discussion of possible models of roles, relationships, functions, procedures and rules.

Consider for example the following project, which concerned a group of occupational therapists and nurses who were employed in a social welfare agency to help assess the needs of the physically handicapped for special aids and for adaptations to their homes. Some considerable degree of antagonism and conflict had grown up between this particular group of staff and the more numerous and dominant body of professional social workers. Originally, the aids and adaptations specialists had worked together from one common base in a central office and under the control of their own principal officer – a situation which had helped to develop considerable *esprit de corps*. Latterly, some had been moved to various local area offices to work alongside professional social workers and under the general aegis of the social-work trained chief area officers. This had been done in order to facilitate better co-ordination and better communication where both they and the professional social workers needed to take action in the same cases.

A further extension of this process was contemplated. The specialists foresaw the increasing physical dispersion of their group as leading inevitably to the destruction of its corporate life. They were concerned that they would lose the technical support of their fellows and their principal officer, that their collective and individual status would be reduced, and that they would find themselves working for new principals who did not really understand the technicalities of their own work. Generally, however, the social workers and area chief officers were in favour of the change. Inevitably tensions grew, and as debate continued comments of an increasingly acid nature about individual attitudes and even capabilities began to emerge.

In the course of social-analytic discussions, these tensions and anxieties were duly noted, but attention was turned towards the underlying structural problems themselves. Efforts were made to find an objective definition of what was meant by 'professional status'. With this achieved, it was easy for all to agree that those of the specialists who warranted such (most of them in fact) would maintain parity of status with professionally qualified social workers wherever they worked. Three precise models of the possible organizational situation of the specialists as regards their simultaneous links with their own principal officer and chief area officer were identified. (The alternative models were similar to those in the situation of administrative staff in area social work offices described earlier in this chapter.) The issue of the actual physical siting of staff was carefully disentangled from that of their organizational control.

With the various structural possibilities exposed in explicit detail, an executive decision was taken which allowed for almost all concerns and anxieties to be met. Responsibility for the actual management of the specialists was firmly and explicitly assigned to their own principal officer. It was confirmed as well that specialists were to retain a common central base so that their prime source of professional and technical support would remain intact. At the same time, whilst recognizing the primacy of the link of specialists to their centrally based team, it was agreed that continued efforts would be made to attach each specialist to outlying area social work offices for part of his time, thus providing him with membership of an additional team, rather than simply transferring him completely. In this way each could spend a significant proportion of his working time in close contact with social work colleagues. However, it was clearly recognized that the role of area chief officers in relation to such attached specialists could be no more than a monitoring or coordinating one.

Thus, by careful analysis of the possibilities of structural clarification, a resolution of many of the basic conflicts was achieved. This was done neither by 'compromise' nor by adopting some diplomatically phrased policy which appeared to satisfy everyone whilst leaving all the real issues untouched. It was done by the teasing out of a detailed formulation or set of formulations, designed to meet the complex realities and multiple needs as they actually were. (As an approach it could also be contrasted, for example, with one which merely helped the various protagonists to become more aware of each other's conflicting feelings and views, or one which encouraged them to make personal adjustments to these conflicts in a more 'mature' way.)

Of course in such situations of overt conflict, or indeed in many others where such conflict is not so manifest, problems may still remain which really are to do with particular people and their attitudes and capabilities. In the course of exploration the social analyst will often find himself faced with comments about personalities, personal capabilities and personal attitudes, particularly where he is in discussion with individuals on their own. On such occasions he may need to remind those with whom he is working that he himself cannot help them with problems that are really and solely personality-based. At the same time, he will point out that if there is a significant doubt or uncertainty on such fundamental things as what work people should be doing, what roles they should properly be playing, and what procedures they ought to be observing, it will be difficult for anyone to make rational judgements about personal capabilities and attitudes. For even where a genuine element of personal inadequacy is thought to be present, until a clear understanding of requisite social institutions has been reached, there is no yardstick against which to make useful judgements of its true extent. There is no means of knowing how far any such personal inadequacy might be met by retraining; or alternatively, of where the inadequate person might be better employed; or again, of exactly what qualities would be demanded of a less inadequate person to fill the same position. Indeed, it might almost be said that in organizational life (as perhaps elsewhere) there is no such thing as an inadequate person, only an inadequate role-performance. Until the terms of the role to be played are clear and agreed, any judgement, sanction or other action must necessarily be premature.

Then again, it is surprising how often so-called 'personality' problems are cut down to size by a thorough-going analysis of prevailing social institutions. Project work has shown so often that what appeared at first sight to be personality clashes is largely to do with wholesale confusion about role and authority, that the importance of clear, well-conceived social structure becomes increasingly impressive. Put in other words, it becomes increasingly evident what diverse kinds of people can happily co-exist and work together in organized groups, given as it were, half a chance!

# 6 Clarifying Language and Concepts

Very high store is set upon clarity of language in social analysis. Without clear and unambiguous language it is not possible to reach understanding about what social problems really involve. Nor is it possible to make precise choices of what to do about them; nor after taking action to know precisely what has worked well and what has not. Nor is it possible to communicate unambiguous information to others about the nature of problems, the action taken to meet them, and its efficacy. In other words, without precise use of language, as in all spheres, there can be no true scientific work carried out; in contrast, say, to journalistic or polemical activity. Thus, in the example quoted in the previous chapter, the analyst is not content to work with phrases such as 'area clerical staff are *under* the Area Officer' or 'area clerical staff are *part* of the Administrative Division'. He demands to know how people interpret words such as the ones stressed here. Where he finds a variety of interpretations and assumptions he looks for more precise language to fall back on, or rather perhaps, to build with. And so too with terms like 'supervising', 'directing', 'controlling', 'deputizing for', 'serving', 'working with', 'providing advice and consultation', 'referring (a case)', 'working as a team', 'reaching a group decision' and many others like them in common use. Which of these can be reclaimed, with explicit definition, as suitable terms for scientific discourse? Which have to be abandoned, for scientific purposes at any rate, as impossible to pin down in any unambiguous meaning? If any have to be abandoned, what can be put in their place?

Social analysis has often been accused by its critics of being trussed in a net of jargon. But in fact, social analysts, unlike for example their colleagues in the natural sciences, have no need for the most part to invent new words. Their concern is social institutions: and the latter, being part of the everyday life of man, already have a very full quota of descriptive language. The aim is not to invent new language nor is it to construct arbitrary definitions. The aim is to clarify language already in use – which means, to clarify the various concepts which the words themselves embody. It is to join in the game of description and theorizing already being undertaken by the actors in the situation in collaboration with them; not to set up a separate 'scientific' discourse parallel to, but separate from, the events of everyday life.[1]

## An Example of Conceptual Clarification – Various Kinds of 'Leaders'

Let us consider some actual examples of conceptual clarification that have taken place in social-analytic work.

In many projects clarification has been necessary of various different meanings implicit in the general notion of one person being 'superior' to another, being 'in charge', being a 'leader'. Early in the Glacier Project for example, in looking at the complex profusion of 'charge hands', 'leading hands', 'setters', 'supervisors', 'assistant foremen', 'foremen' and 'superintendents' in that manufacturing concern, two basic conceptions were teased out – that of a *manager* and that of a *supervisor*.[2] A *manager* was one who carried full accountability for the work of those whom he led. He was expected to be able to make effective assessments of his subordinates' capacities, and to assign duties to them accordingly. He was expected to appraise their performance, to help them develop in their work, and to recommend appropriate financial advancement or promotion. In extreme cases, he would be expected to make the judgement that a person was unsuitable for any work within his own domain, and thus to have authority to initiate the transfer of the person concerned elsewhere.

By contrast, a *supervisor* would not have authority to make such major decisions – and could therefore not be held accountable to the same degree for the work of those whom he controlled. His role

---

[1] In a sense, social analysis might be described as 'applied ethnomethodology'. For a description of the ethnomethodological approach in sociology, *see* Douglas (1970), *Understanding Everyday Life*; Turner (1974), *Ethnomethodology*. However, as noted in Chapter 4, social analysis, unlike ethnomethodology and similar sociological undertakings, is concerned with facilitating change, not simply with generating greater understanding.

[2] See *Exploration in Management*, Chapter 14.

would encompass more specific things such as inducting new staff, assigning specific pieces of work to them (of the kind that the manager had indicated as suitable), and helping them with work problems; although he would have the right to pass his comments to the manager on the general performance of those whom he supervised. Abolition of the various previous titles and the confused roles which they carried with them, and the re-allocation of staff concerned either to full managerial roles or to supervisory roles, according to personal ability paved the way to a markedly simpler and more socially effective structure.

In the course of the health services work described in the case-study in Chapter 2, a further conception of a 'leader' or 'leading' role emerged. This was the conception of the *co-ordinator*.[3] The latter carried significantly less authority, and therefore less accountability, than either the manager or the supervisor. He would have no rights to make or transmit personal judgements on those he co-ordinated, let alone to concern himself with their long-term development and careers. Nor would he have the right to set rules or policies which were binding upon them, as would a manager. His role would include such things as producing detailed programmes, issuing detailed instructions and checking on progress, all within the framework of already given policies and agreed objectives.

The distinction of a co-ordinative role from a managerial one (and of both from the 'monitoring' role described in the same case-study in Chapter 2) played a major part in helping to formulate appropriate plans for the detailed managerial structure of the reorganized National Health Service, introduced in 1974.[4]

Also in the health services work, further conceptual clarification became necessary in considering the roles of certain doctors in leading positions such as 'chief medical officers', 'superintendent physicians', 'chief pathologists' and 'senior surgeons'. All these were obviously in some sort of leadership role to their fellow doctors, but there was a crucial divide to be recognized. On the one hand, there were those who could be best conceived as appointed officers. In some cases these could be seen as carrying out a *co-ordinative* role in respect of their clinical colleagues, and in others a *managerial* role. In both cases however, they would be accountable to their employers for such work. On the other hand, there were doctors who were best conceived not as appointed officers, but as elected *representatives*,

---

[3] See *Hospital Organization*, pp. 47–9.

[4] *See* Department of Health and Social Security (1972), *Management Arrangements for the Reorganized Health Service*.

ultimately accountable only to their colleagues who elected them, and with the duty of forwarding the general views and interests of these same colleagues rather than that of the employing authority, should there be a difference between the two.[5]

## Clarification of 'Teamwork' and 'Referral' Conceptions

Let us consider a further example of conceptual clarification of a very different kind, which arose from project work with those involved in the 'child guidance' field.

One of the things on which emphasis had always been placed in this field was the need for close multi-disciplinary work which brought together the various skills of such people as psychiatrists, educational psychologists, social workers and child psychotherapists, in dealing with the problems of disturbed children and their families. Much weight in discussion and writing had always been given to the desirability of 'teamwork'. But was 'teamwork' always what was required? Analysis of various practice situations disclosed not just one, but two possible conceptions. One of these might truly be called 'teamwork'. The other might be better described as a 'network' situation.[6]

A true teamwork conception implied very close working together and high personal confidence. It implied, for example, that newcomers to established teams must be personally acceptable to existing members and that they must be willing to adhere to established norms and practices. It implied that there would be frequent face-to-face interaction for the team as a whole, and that all accredited members would be free to attend and join in any general team meetings.

Such a mode of organization might generate high standards of work, but clearly it would be highly demanding of staff numbers and of staff time. Sometimes there would simply not be enough resources of all kinds of staff to allow the establishment of full multi-disciplinary teams in every site. However, the alternative was not necessarily a situation in which individuals would have to work on

---

[5] See *Hospital Organization*, Chapters 5, 6 and 12. The concept of elected 'representative' had of course been clearly identified in previous Glacier Project work – see *Exploration in Management*, Chapter 16. *See also* Newman and Rowbottom (1968), *Organization Analysis*, pp. 91–2, and Jaques (1976), *A General Theory of Bureaucracy*, Chapter 19.

[6] *See* Brunel Institute of Organization and Social Studies (1976a), *Future Organization in Child Guidance and Allied Work, A Working Paper*.

their own with no interaction with other professionals. It would often be possible, and indeed desirable, to establish strong 'networks' of interaction between professionals of various kinds, even if they were not working together all the time. Particular individuals in specific agencies could be nominated as regular 'contacts'; staff from different agencies or disciplines could be placed in adjacent premises in order to facilitate communication; 'liaison' posts could be established; and so on. In this alternative conception it would not be necessary as it would in full-scale teamwork for the acceptability of newcomers to be tested with all other potential interacting professionals. Nor would regular face-to-face meetings of full network groups be essential; nor would the agreement of one individual or group to respect the accepted norms and practices of all other established individuals and groups.

Another area where great need for painstaking conceptual analysis has revealed itself in child guidance work, as well as in many other fields where health and social services professionals regularly work together, is around the notion of the 'referral' of cases from one practitioner to another. Many practical problems can arise from different interpretations of the significance of this term. If, for example, general medical practitioners refer patients who are in beds which they themselves control in cottage hospitals, to specialist consultants, does the case then belong to the GP or the consultant? If a surgeon refers a case to a physiotherapist for treatment, does the case now pass to the latter? If a social worker in a specially created 'intake' team in a social welfare agency refers a case to another social worker in one of the 'long-term' teams in the same agency, does this mean that responsibility automatically transfers with the act of referral?

In such situations analysis has revealed at least three distinct meanings or conceptions.[7] The first meaning is that of referral for a possible *transfer* of responsibility for the work, given the agreement of the person referred to. The second is that of referral for possible *collaboration*, again with the agreement of the person referred to. (And here the further question then follows of who will take prime responsibility for the work.) In a third situation, 'referral' does not imply either a request for transfer or for collaboration. What is happening is that the referrer is really giving an authoritative *prescription* for certain subsidiary work to be carried out in order to help him with his continuing professional task. These various distinctions

[7] *See* Brunel Institute of Organization and Social Studies (1976a), (1976b), (1977.)

and conceptions have now been used with benefit in innumerable actual projects in the health and social services field.

## Clarification of the Idea of 'Responsibility'

We might take as a final example of conceptual clarification one concerning a deeper and more general idea, namely that of 'responsibility'. Careful analysis demonstrates a whole cluster of conceptual distinctions here, all relevant to various specific practical issues.

What is the responsibility of a person at work? One sense of the word – sometimes denoted as 'responsibilities' in the plural – is the things that people in particular positions are expected to do. Closer analysis of this particular usage distinguishes in fact two further sub-concepts. First there is the conception of *duty*, as a continuing obligation to perform activities of a particular kind, associated with a particular social position. Secondly there is the conception of *task*, the idea of a specific piece of work, with a specific end-point to be achieved within some explicit or implicit time limit. The examination of this particular aspect of responsibility – the idea of specific tasks – was in fact instrumental in revealing a link between the longest tasks likely to arise in a particular organizational position (the so-called 'time-span of discretion') and a yet further conception of responsibility namely the felt burden or weight of responsibility associated with the job (as indicated in usages like 'it is a very responsible job' or 'he carries a lot of responsibility').[8]

Yet another conception of responsibility is *sense of responsibility*; that is, a personal characteristic which may or may not be possessed by a particular person. Another still, is the idea of *accountability*, which is simply the likelihood to be held to account and to be praised, blamed or otherwise rewarded or sanctioned for activities undertaken in a particular social position.[9] The distinction between these last two meanings is particularly useful in exploring with professional people like social workers, doctors or nurses for example, what things they are responsible for. To ask them all the things they feel a sense of responsibility about is one thing. To ask them more precisely what their perception is of the things for which they are specifically accountable in their particular posts provides different and instructive answers.

Thus in undertaking social analysis, the necessity for the clarification of language and concept may arise in a variety of spheres and at

[8] *See* Jaques (1967), *Equitable Payment*.
[9] *See* Newman and Rowbottom (1968), *Organization Analysis*, pp. 25–7.

a number of different levels of generality. Over the course of the years a wide range of precise and distinct conceptions of relationship types in organized activity has emerged: managerial, supervisory, staff, monitoring, co-ordinating, representative, service-giving and so on.[10] A number of concepts concerning procedures and interactive processes of various kinds have also emerged. There is for example the distinction of 'legislative' and 'appeals' processes in industrial relations which was established in the Glacier Project.[11] There is the whole family of concepts underlying the broad ideas of 'case responsibility' and 'referral' in multi-disciplinary interaction between doctors, nurses, social workers, therapists and so on, in health and social welfare settings, to which we have just briefly referred.[12] At a deeper level, there is the work which has been done on attempting to clarify such fundamental social conceptions as those of work, responsibility, authority, social power, employment and profession.[13]

## Finding Viable Terms

As we have said, social analysis is not attempting the artificial production of new jargon terms or the elaboration of definitions for their own sake and however arbitrary. It is concerned with the language of social institutions already in everyday employment, and with clarifying the various conceptions which it embodies. The quest is to identify amongst the host of words already used by the prime actors in the situation those of key importance. It is to tease out the most incisive and significant meanings of these, so that they can be used as precise instruments of thinking and negotiation, rather than remaining as vague tokens in a largely ritual exchange.

If at all possible, the precise conceptions reclaimed should be given names already in use. Only if no suitable commonplace terms exist should resort be made to out-of-the-ordinary ones or (worse still) to neologisms – artificial words.

The terms chosen must ideally be such that, singled out for special attention and precise definition, they are readily seen to be usable and useful by the actors in the situation, and therefore adopted for immediate employment in their everyday deliberations. Such terms

[10] See *Social Services Departments*, Appendix A, and Jaques (1976), *A General Theory of Bureaucracy*, Chapters 4, 17 and 19.
[11] See *Exploration in Management*, Chapters 17 and 18.
[12] *See* Brunel Institute of Organization and Social Studies (1976a), (1976b), (1977).
[13] Further discussions and appropriate references are offered in Chapter 8.

were 'representative', 'manager' and (by distinction) 'supervisor' in the Glacier Project; or 'co-ordinator' and 'monitor' as defined in the Health Services Project. Such slightly out-of-the-ordinary terms as 'collateral' (for a genuine relationship of give-and-take equality between two organizational colleagues) or 'co-management' (in the sense described in the case-study in the previous chapter) have been widely adopted and used too, because they conveyed some reasonably apparent meaning that was commonly needed to be expressed in organizational situations.

Sometimes however, the analyst misjudges. For example the term 'conjoint' for the relationships of several interacting staff-officers at any given organizational point, suggested at one stage in the Glacier Project[14] has never really 'taken'. Nor has the term 'functional monitoring and co-ordinating' for one possible relationship between specialist staffs at various organizational levels suggested at one stage in the Health Services Project.[15]

## Clarification of Basic Functions to be Performed

A significant portion of the effort in social-analytic work in practice then is taken up with conceptual clarifications of the kinds just described – clarification of various kinds of social relationships in organized groups, clarifications of various kinds of procedure, clarification of more basic social ideas. With these basic building-blocks to hand, more complex models or formulations can readily be constructed which remain clear and unambiguous however extended or detailed they may become.

At this point however, an urgent question may present itself. Is there not an element missing? Can it ever be proper to go ahead with the formulation of organizational models, however clear the concepts in which they are framed, without some specific consideration of the *objectives* to be pursued?

The answer to these questions in fact itself necessitates a piece of conceptual clarification in respect of the word 'objective'. This word has, of course, many more or less exact synonyms – goals, tasks, targets, end-products, objects, aims, policies, functions and so on. Without attempting to attach a special meaning to each, a fundamental distinction can be drawn between the kind of value words which relate to social institutions on the one hand, and those which

[14] See *Exploration in Management*, Chapter 15.
[15] See *Hospital Organization*, Chapter 4.

relate to 'programming' or 'technical' issues (as defined in Chapter 3) on the other. The distinction is of considerable practical importance.

We have already introduced a term to stand for statements of value or aim implicit in social institutions: that term is 'function'. All statements of function have a particular grammatical form (or can readily be cast in a form) which describes an activity which indefinitely continues: 'helping families in distress', 'providing maternity services', 'developing, manufacturing, and selling bearings' and so on. Programmatic value terms on the other hand, take quite a different form, implying as they do specific, time-related pieces of work – 'take this child into care', 'put up a new maternity wing', 'shift business from metal to plastic bearings', etc. Technical goals too, have a distinctive form – 'produce specific goods or services of this particular kind or specification'.

The point is that it is no part of institutional analysis to analyse either programme goals or technical goals. These are (as discussed in Chapter 3) within fields of analysis in their own right, and demand different modes of exploration, different approaches and different skills. The proper starting place of all analysis of social institutions is precisely the analysis of functions to be undertaken. Programme or technical goals will only influence social institutions to the extent that they alter the nature of the basic functions to be performed.

In fact, it is quite impossible to carry out any piece of social analysis, however circumscribed, without some analysis and clarification of functions to be performed: the only issue is how broadly the analysis is pitched. Even the specification of a particular kind of institutionalized relationship between the occupants of two posts or positions, A and B, necessarily involves some specification of the functions to be carried out by A in relation to B, or vice versa. Thus, in the case-study of the three senior hospital officers described in Chapter 2, the basic issues were things like: what functions is the Group Secretary required to perform on behalf of the Hospital Management Committee; what functions has the Treasurer necessarily to perform in his role as monitor of expenditure? And in the case-study of administrative staff in an area social work office discussed in Chapter 5, they were things like: what functions is it appropriate for the Area Officer to carry out as the senior person in regular contact with the administrative staff concerned and as the prime user of their services; what functions should the Chief Administrator at Central Office perform in order to give them necessary support and technical control?

More broadly pitched projects allow of course a more fundamental analysis of functional requirements. An analysis of the operational functions of the Glacier Metal Company (typical in this respect of all manufacturing companies, no doubt) showed that these necessarily included three independent though interacting elements: a manufacturing activity, a product development activity, and a marketing or selling activity. From this it was possible to deduce the general form of organizational structure needed to carry them out.[16] In a general exploration of the child guidance service undertaken at Brunel, analysis showed that radically different organizational models would be called for depending on how the function to be performed in connection with the problems of disturbed children and their families was conceived. One view would conceive it as the treatment of 'mental illness' and thus as part of a comprehensive health service. A second would be to conceive it as the prevention and alleviation of 'social distress', and thus as part of comprehensive social welfare services. A third would see it as dealing with 'educational' problems. A fourth would see it as attempting to deal with all those things comprehensively and at the same time.[17] (Increasingly in recent years the work at Brunel, heavily oriented as it has been to the public service sector, has been drawn into analysis of such fundamental social concepts as 'health care', 'mental health care', 'welfare', 'education', 'therapy' and the like, and the distinctions between them.)

Social analysis then, like all other rational analysis of human activity, has necessarily to go back in the end to consideration of ultimate goals. However, being concerned with the development of social institutions, these goals typically become re-expressed as the 'functions' which the institutions are required, or desired, to perform. Consideration of the specific, time-bounded objectives which are to be pursued, even though they must certainly be consistent with institutional functions, is another matter – what was described in Chapter 3 as a 'programming' one. So too is any consideration of technical criteria or specifications.

---

[16] *Exploration in Management*, Chapter 11.

[17] Brunel Institute of Organization and Social Studies (1976a), *Future Organization in Child Guidance and Allied Work, A Working Paper.*

# 7 Practical Procedure

In the two previous chapters we have seen that the actual process of collaborative exploration in social analysis centres round a careful 'teasing out' of possible requisite institutions from the complex of manifest statements, experienced problems, working assumptions and underlying needs that may exist at any time in any given situation. The concern of the analyst himself is not with simply proferring solutions, but with helping to lay bare formulations in general terms of the various possible models, and their respective implications and consequences. He is not there to advise, but to elucidate.

In order to produce clear, explicit and testable formulations, much attention has to be given to clarification of basic concepts behind everyday descriptions of organized social life: terms such as 'responsibility', 'leadership', 'referral', 'consultation', 'team-work' and innumerable others like them. Analysis and clarification of the particular functions to be performed in the setting concerned will invariably need to be undertaken as well.

Having established some idea of the essence of the work in practice, we may now consider the actual step-by-step procedure in mounting and following through social-analytic projects.

### Establishing Initial Contact

How the initial contact is made with potential collaborators depends largely on the existing position of the social analyst. Where he is already well established in a particular field, the initiative may be taken by would-be collaborators themselves, following perhaps word-of-mouth recommendation, or their attendance at a conference, seminar or talk, in which the social analyst has figured. Where on the other hand, the social analyst is starting up business in some new field of work then he himself will probably have to take the initiative. He may start by making approaches in what appear to be a number of likely venues for work, and explaining to the people there the kind of collaboration that is possible should they wish to respond. Particularly where the field of work is new to him, the analyst will in any case be concerned with some preliminary exercise of self-education. He will want to read as much as possible of the relevant literature, scan the periodicals, contact other established researchers or activists in the field, and perhaps even arrange a series of impression-gathering visits to representative sites and institutions. In the course of these, valuable personal contacts may be made which later yield invitations for full-scale social analysis.

However, there is always a danger where the analyst has made the initial approach, whether for the purpose of gathering information and impressions, or in order to canvass directly the possibility of social-analytic work. The danger is that any proposals which do emerge are perceived as being for some kind of more conventional, researcher-initiated, 'objective' study – albeit dressed up (for some perhaps not altogether clear reason) in participative clothing. Where things start like this, there is the imminent likelihood of being confronted at some later point with that most damaging of remarks for the social analyst – 'now, exactly what do you want us to tell you?' (A good working test for whether in the event the researcher has been helping those with whom he is in contact, or *vice versa*, that is whether or not true collaborative exploration has taken place, is who says 'thank you' at the end of the discussion!)

In practice, as might be expected, it is usually one of the more influential figures in any organized group who makes initial contact, or with whom contact is made. In hierarchic organizations it is likely to be either the head or one of his or her immediate subordinates. In collegial-type organizations such as are to be found in groupings of independent professionals, in formal associations of various kinds, or in various kinds of governing bodies and committees, it is likely to be the chairman, a committee member or one of the other leading lights.

Thereafter several different kinds of situations may emerge. Sometimes the contact may prompt the thought of enlisting the help of the analyst in a renewed attack on a long-standing problem which has so far resisted all internal efforts to reduce it. We might cite here as an example, the long-standing problem of the deputy in a research and testing organization described at the start of Chapter 3.

In a second kind of situation, a designated task-group or working party may already be at work on some organizational issue, and the analyst may be invited to contribute to it. This happened when social analysts at Brunel were invited to join a national working party established by the Department of Health to propose detailed organizational arrangements for the reorganized National Health Service which was to be introduced in 1974. It happened in another instance where analysts from Brunel were invited to join a group of four directors of social services in the East Sussex region who were jointly engaged in producing proposals for the organization of a new unified department, in preparation for the coming merger of their four local authorities.

In a third and rather more rare kind of situation, discussions may move directly to the possibilities of entering into a lasting relationship, in which a continuing series of projects may be embarked upon as the needs arise. Such a situation arose at the start of the Glacier Project, outlined in Chapter 1.

Of course, these are just the situations as they initially appear and things may change radically thereafter. What was initially conceived as work on one specific project may eventually grow into a more permanent relationship. Conversely, what may have been foreseen initially as the beginning of a permanent relationship may often in the event fail to develop. In all cases however, before actual social-analytic work can start in earnest on any particular project, there are important preliminaries to be undertaken.

## Preliminary Discussions

At an early point there will, for a start, be need for consideration of financial arrangements. The organization concerned may itself be willing to find the money or contribute a major share of it. In the public sector, central government agencies may be willing to fund the work. Research councils or research-sponsoring private trusts may perhaps be approached.

The social analyst will need to have a number of preliminary meetings with various groups of members of the body or organization concerned. A start may be made perhaps by meeting a broad selection of senior or representative staff. Then a second meeting may be arranged with the leading members particularly concerned with the specific project proposed. This may be followed perhaps by a third with a more extended group of people directly concerned.

In all these preliminary meetings the task of the social analyst is to expound and explain the particular nature of his approach, and to test that certain specific preconditions for social-analytic work exist.

First, he must confirm that the problems proposed for study do in fact have a significant institutional element; that is, that they have to do with the general way people are organized or work together, however this may be or appear to be compounded with other things such as 'personality difficulties'. For if it turns out that there is no reason to think that exploration will reveal any significant problems with the social institutions themselves, then there is no role for the social analyst whatever there may be for other kinds of researcher or consultant.

Second, he must check that there is enough concern about these problems for people to want to devote time and energy to doing something about them. The answer to the question (often posed) 'how much time will all this study take?' is (firmly) 'just as much, or as little, as you wish to give it, bearing in mind all the other demands on you'. If the 'problems' are not such that people could spare much time to attending to them, the real message is obvious.

Third, the analyst must make it clear that he will not be proffering specific advice or recommendations, but merely helping to analyse problems and expose possibilities. Here the analyst will stress that in order to leave the way open for the freest and frankest exploration of issues he will treat each and every discussion as confidential. Control of what material is released for further and broader discussion, or eventually perhaps for general publication, will rest completely in the hands of the person or people concerned. It will be pointed out that one possible consequence of this promise of confidentiality is that the organization or body as a whole (let alone any sponsoring bodies, or the interested public) might never know what transpired in a particular project or part-project if the person or people concerned preferred at the end of the day not to give clearance for release of any of the material discussed. (It may be observed in passing that once discussions are finally underway, people usually appear remarkably free, in fact, in taking the analyst into their confidence,[1] and remarkably willing to release material.)

Overall, he must emphasize that there has to be a high degree of willingness to undertake exploration with the analyst. Of course, any

---

[1] It is the author's personal observation that this is also true of approaches used by many management consultants or the like, even where the various principles of collaboration and confidentiality described above are not adopted. However, only too often the capital of confidence thus initially created is rapidly and disastrously dissipated when, at a later stage, respondents discover that the consultant has added new impressions or interpretations, as well as his own personal advice or criticism, in retailing reports of discussion to higher authorities.

kind of social research or interaction requires some degree of cooperation from those involved. However in social analysis there must be willingness to join in positive collaboration, not just willingness to provide information or views. Any idea of coerced or directed cooperation ('my boss has told me to cooperate with you – all right, what do you want to know?') quite rules out the possibility of effective, creative work. Each individual is free to decide for himself whether to join in, and is free to withdraw at any time.

What it is not the job of the analyst to do in these preliminary meetings is to expound the problem which is considered to exist, let alone to press in any way that urgent attention be given to it. In order to deal with this issue it is therefore essential that one of the leading members who are initiating or sponsoring the particular proposal also attend each such preparatory meeting. For the analyst to attempt to combine the task of explaining his own possible role, with that of even simply reporting the project proposals made by other leading organization members who are not present, has frequently been shown to lead to disaster. These preparatory discussions are the most complex and difficult, in social terms, in the whole social-analytic process. The essence of a subtle and unusual approach has to be conveyed to an unprepared and, in many cases, diverse group of people. Opportunities for misunderstanding are rife. Suspicion is often high (though not always voiced). It is by no means unknown for general sanction to fail at this stage. The analyst has enough to do without courting confusion by attempting to play the role of initiator and advocate in addition to his own.

On the other hand, if this first barrier is surmounted, the particular conditions in which social-analytic work is carried out make it rare thereafter to encounter any significant hostility or sustained emotional opposition from those actually participating – in contrast to what is often experienced in more prescriptive approaches. At the worst, projects simply die out. This may happen for example because of some externally imposed reorganization or change of policy. Or it may happen because of the departure of some key figure who has been sponsoring the project. Or it may simply happen because for some reason the analyst has failed to grapple effectively with the real problem besetting the actors immediately concerned, so that their interest gradually flags.

## Subsequent Steps in Project Work

The pattern of work which usually follows these preliminary meetings, assuming that they do indeed result in general agreement to proceed, can now be described.

In early social-analytic practice up to about 1952, actual project discussions were almost entirely conducted in groups. This (as discussed in the first chapter) was the time at which the interpretation was still predominantly psychological in nature. Thereafter, the practice grew, and now remains standard, of starting with individual discussions, then returning to group discussion at a later point. Elliott Jaques' own statement of the reasons for the shift in practice are interesting and persuasive:

> In a group, each person is strongly influenced by his ideas of how the opinions of the others present will be affected towards him by what he says. He is inevitably conscious how his words will affect their judgement. His career may be affected. Or certainly his position in his own group may be. Or, by speaking about others, he may somehow damage them. He has to be extremely careful about what he says. Thus, for example, a manager may become quite anxious about expressing tentative ideas in front of his subordinates in case they take them by default as his point of view . . .
>
> By contrast, private discussion in a social-analytic setting has a very different character. The individual is free to think out loud. It is an unusual and rare situation. The social-analyst can feed back what he is saying, can analyse it, can help to make explicit what is only implicit, can help to take other factors into account. But he is not sitting in judgement on the individual or his views. He is not setting up his own particular opposition line or policy. He will not report anything from the discussion, except that which the person subsequently desires.[2]

Usually the chance of individual discussions will be offered to all the actors who have been involved in the preliminaries described above. Sometimes however the sheer numbers of people concerned makes it necessary to explore problems with a representative sample rather than with all. In this case the final choice of the appropriate sample will, of course, rest with the group concerned, though the analyst is not debarred from contributing any thoughts on the subject which he may have. Each individual discussion typically extends over one or two hours. Shorter sessions tend not to allow time to penetrate to the deeper layers of the problems to be explored, whilst

[2] Jaques (1965c), pp. 44–5.

longer ones become too fatiguing. However, as little as half an hour might serve for those peripherally involved in a problem. Sometimes one such discussion suffices initially: sometimes two or more are required.

Following such discussions the analyst will draft notes of the ground covered and conclusions reached, and present them to the person with whom he has held the discussion. Each report typically includes an analysis of the organizational problems explored, together with some factual background information, and perhaps some first tentative sketches of requisite institutional models and their implications. (*See* the specimen reports in Appendix A.) This draft may be acceptable as it stands. Often however some degree of amendment is required, if only for factual accuracy. Sometimes seeing the actual expression of ideas in writing stimulates the recipient to ask for further discussion and exploration. The aim at this stage is to see if a written statement can be produced which can be drawn on with confidence by both the analyst and the person he has been working with, in providing material for the group discussions to come.

Although it is usual to produce a written report for each discussion or set of discussions with any one individual, it is possible on occasion to omit this step and move straight to the production of a more general report for the whole group, of the kind to be described below. This may be done where, for instance, there is a relatively large number of people involved in the project, with perhaps a large degree of similarity of role or concern. It may be the most suitable course where there is strong pressure to get to a group discussion in a relatively short period of time. What is lost with such a short-cut however, is precisely the possibility just described, of generating in the individual collaborator further ideas stimulated by his seeing on paper the analysis that has emerged from discussion so far.

Having had private discussions with all the individuals who wished to contribute, and having cleared written material with each of them, the analyst will now prepare a document which summarizes and generalizes the issues as they appear at this stage (*see* Specimen 2 in Appendix A). He will then circulate this to all the people identified as part of the original project group, in preparation for a first group project discussion. He may also circulate at the same time all the individual reports which have been cleared, if this seems appropriate. Otherwise he will simply indicate that they are available for those who wish to see them. Given the careful and detailed preparatory work of the individual discussion, and the availability of a written document which offers explicit statements which can be debated as they stand, the group as a whole is now in a good position to do creative work. The analyst will join freely in the ensuing general discussion, whilst holding firm to his analytic posture. To the extent that stage-management or chairmanship of the meeting is required, the responsibility must rest with the organization members themselves, rather than the analyst. (This may be contrasted with the position of the analyst in 'research conferences' which is to be discussed below.)

This last point will bear some elaboration. Within such meetings it might seem at first sight desirable to put existing authority-relationships on one side. But this of course is not really possible. It is necessary to accept and work with the existing social structure, whatever it may be. Thus, where a clear institutional superior is present, although it may be hoped that he avoids arbitrary use of his authority in dealing with the substance of the matters in hand, he is nevertheless the obvious person to 'lead' or 'chair' the meeting in terms of pace, procedure, proposals for next steps and so on. Where a group of peers is involved, the group themselves must find their own chairman, even if only for the occasion concerned.

Following this general principle of the recognition of the realities of existing organizational authority, experience has also shown the wisdom of letting any superiors or managers who may exist in a situation have a preliminary discussion of the general report with the analyst. If those who are going to lead group discussions do not have this chance, they are faced in the actual session with a double task. Not only do they have to try and ensure that the group is led as effectively as possible; over and above this they have at the same time the job of coming to terms themselves with new and perhaps somewhat difficult ideas, and formulating their own personal reactions to them.

Invariably in a first discussion with the full group, further ideas are generated, some possibilities eliminated or refined, or some new ones identified. Further group meetings may well be felt to be necessary. At some stage a revised report can be produced, which may in turn stimulate further discussion.

Finally, a time is reached where this particular group have clarified their ideas to the point that they may now wish to elicit the reaction of some broader group, or those in some position of higher authority to them. Since the accumulated analysis, and the ideas on which it is based, will be unfamiliar to any new people coming into the project, careful introductory work and interpretation will be necessary in order to let them catch up. In the course of discussions, these newcomers too will naturally offer their own impressions and ideas of the subject, and it will be up to the analyst to incorporate any important new elements which emerge in a further written exposition. Thus, all the time, he will be conscious of being immersed in a continuing process of changing perception and evolving insight, rather than one in which certain objective 'data', and the conclusions which have been drawn from it, are discussed in unchanging form in a sequence of different settings.

Assuming that the enactment of organizational change of some kind is now determined upon, those members of the body or organization who are proposing it will themselves have to take steps to explain what is proposed and to get sanction for it in the usual way. The analyst can sometimes make a contribution by helping to disseminate understanding of the issues concerned, and of the reasons for change, through specially arranged seminars or conferences (*see* below). However, it is not part of his role to advocate the particular changes proposed, or in any way to act as part of the chain of decision or implementation.

Beyond this point the further involvement of the analyst will be less predictable. In some instances it is specifically arranged that a formal review of the effect and effectiveness of the changes will take place after a given period of time (as in the case-study described in Chapter 2) – say three or six months. In this case it is very likely that the social analyst will be asked to become actively involved again when the review takes place. More usually (for reasons which will be explored in Chapter 9) no such formal arrangement is made. The people concerned are left to get on with things and only if they specifically discover shortcomings in the new arrangements is the question of the analyst's further involvement likely to be raised. Where he is for any reason invited to become involved again, even in a formal 'evaluation' process, his role remains simply that of elucidating new problems that have arisen and helping to formulate possibilities for further alleviation and change. He does not assume any new role as a detached scientific observer, a collector of 'objective' evidence, or an independent evaluator (an important point that will again need elaboration later).

## Continuity of Work and Links with the Whole of the Social Entity Concerned

Even if the social analyst is not invited to return to some area of work in connection with the project with which he was originally involved, there are good reasons why he may hope if at all possible to undertake work on further projects with the same people or with their immediate colleagues or fellows. For in order for the social-analytic process to give of its best and fullest fruits, two conditions are required. The first is that links with the organization or body concerned shall continue in existence over long periods of time. The second is that the linkage with the body concerned shall be as comprehensive as possible.

As far as continuity is concerned, the analyst may hope ideally to keep on working with particular groups with whom he has established contact for periods of time stretching to many years. The more the social analyst is imbued with the outlook of his collaborators, the more, that is, he can move freely in their particular world and see it and its dilemmas through their eyes, the more likely he is to do good work (though this, of course, is not in itself a sufficient condition). Without the depth of insight that only continued contact can bring, the chance of producing genuine new scientific advances is slim indeed. How often has the social analyst looked back with a shudder to his first fumbling attempts at formulation in some new field of work! If only a pattern of continual contact can be established with a particular group or body, a pattern in which enacted change follows analysis, and in which subsequent problems are further analysed, leading to further corrective action (the sort of cycle described in the case-study in Chapter 2), work of quite a different quality and authority results. Only by continuity does social analysis achieve its ultimate goal – the accumulation of scientific knowledge, which has been tried and tested in deliberate change.

Again, the more comprehensive the range of projects entered into with those in any distinct social entity or body, and the greater the extent of involvement with people in all parts and at all levels of the body concerned, the greater the chance of achieving a comprehensive and unbiased view of the various constituent institutions which are necessary. Here 'social entity' may imply something as small as a particular factory, office or hospital, or something as large as a complete nationwide business. Only exploration in each case will establish the extent and limits of the grouping of people who feel themselves to be an integral part of some distinct social whole.

Often the feeling of being part of one distinct entity will be based on the frequent interaction within one contained geographical site of all those concerned – common membership, that is, of an 'institution' in the more concrete sense of the word.

There is another reason too for seeking to establish as comprehensive a relationship as possible with the total membership of the distinct social entity concerned, whatever it may be. As was observed in the previous chapter it is usual for initial contact in project work to be made with a leading or dominant group of people in the organization or body concerned. Inevitably it is they who are likely to take the initiative of sponsoring projects in the first instance, and also in defining what does, or does not, constitute 'problems'. The task for the social analyst is to move over time to a situation where he is perceived not just by the leadership, the élite, as an available source of help, but as far as possible by all those who are members of the body concerned.

This does not imply that he could ever achieve a state where he was receiving invitations equally from members of all kinds, regardless of level or influence. Such an image is simply unrealistic. Inevitably, any of those that sponsor suggestions for unusual work of the kind in view here are likely to be out of the run-of-the-mill: the activists or initiators in their circle, however small. Most, in the natural course of things, will already have reached some position of formally acknowledged leadership – 'shop-steward', 'chairman', 'section head' or whatever.

Nevertheless, the broader the range of relationships established, the better. In the Glacier Project, for example, social-analytic work has been undertaken with shop-floor and clerical staff as well as with top- and middle-level managers; with salesmen, production staff and research and development staff; and with a range of elected staff representatives and union officials. In work with some particular hospitals and social welfare agencies a similar diversity of contact has been closely approach, if not yet perhaps quite equalled.

Where extensive links with a complete social group or entity are developed over time, not only does the social analyst have a much better chance of developing a realistic, comprehensive and unbiased view of the social realities concerned. There is also a greater likelihood that useful institutional change will take place. Indeed in the most desirable case, what might be thought of as a basic shift in the general culture of the body concerned may start to manifest itself. A climate of opinion may gradually emerge in which it is taken for granted that all kinds of social problems and conflicts may benefit from careful conceptual analysis and definition. It may gradually come to be accepted that a truly scientific approach to institutional development is a thing to be pursued, not only through the help of an external social analyst, but by every thinking individual for himself and with his fellows.[3]

## Use of Conferences and Seminars

One of the ways in which the roots of social-analytic work in a particular setting, or indeed in a whole range of similar settings, can be extended and strengthened, is through the running of research-linked conferences and seminars. The precise aims of such events can be summed up in two words: *testing* and *dissemination*.

Firstly, conferences give a unique opportunity to test the adequacy and usefulness of more general concepts and formulations which may be emerging from a number of similar projects being undertaken at any time. Admittedly the 'test' here, which is simply one of concentrated discussion, and appeal to collective experience, is very different from the test through enacted change in specific social situations. But it is nevertheless an invaluable supplement to project work. It gives the chance for the social analyst to piece together perhaps fragmentary and slowly developing ideas from a number of separate field projects, and to explore them systematically in a way which is much more under his direct control. Moreover, it provides a unique chance to test or pre-test the true generality of emerging findings. (In this respect the conference makes an important contribution to the scientific aspect of social analysis, which is to be discussed in the next chapter.)

The second function, integrally linked, is the dissemination of case material, models and theories. Here conferences can be useful in reinforcing executive action resulting from project work, drawing members from those more or less directly involved in the actual changes, in the specific setting concerned. Useful preparatory work can also be done with people from other settings where social-analytic work is about to be started for the first time, or where it is contemplated as a possibility. There is also scope for work with

---

[3] In these circumstances the social analyst might be thought of as having moved from the role of helping to analyse specific problems to that of a general *educator*. How far and how fast it is appropriate to move deliberately to a broader educative role in any one piece of project work is another matter however, and one strongly related to the needs and capabilities of the particular people being worked with. *See* Dale (1974), 'Coercive Persuasion and the Role of the Change Agent', on some of these points.

'activists' from a broader area – senior executives, senior personnel officers, up-and-coming younger people, academics, publicists, leading professionals and the like – drawn from a regional, national, or even international audience. The aim here is to reach people who have the ability to take some of the general products of social-analytic work in the field concerned and make use of them in their specific working situations, even without the direct support of collaborative project work.

The correct label for such events constitutes a problem in itself, to which a satisfactory answer has not yet been found. Practice has favoured 'conference'; though the normal usage of the term carries implications of a gathering in which many speakers make formal contributions, often from varying theoretical viewpoints, which is not the case here. The word 'seminar' carries a flavour of teaching or deliberate instruction, which is not suitable. The word 'course' is quite wide of what is intended. (Social analysts may however in other distinct roles as lecturers within teaching institutions, or as trainers of would-be social analysts, undertake clear teaching and seminar work.)

Appropriate membership will be readily indicated by the particular purpose of the event. A project-related conference will naturally call for as many as possible of the group directly concerned with the project in hand, regardless of exact grade, seniority, experience or intellectual capacity. At the other extreme, a conference drawing on a regional or national audience, and concerned with some more general topic, will be aiming to recruit members of sufficient experience and ability to be able to comprehend and internalize the ideas being presented, and with sufficient influence to make effective use of them at some future date.

In conferences as such, authority relationships between members will not however be a crucial matter. Even in project-linked conferences the exercise is simply concerned with increasing knowledge or understanding in some way, and not in itself with solving problems or initiating enacted change. The event is one which is specifically designed, co-ordinated and led by the analyst. In sharp contrast to his role in project work, in the conference or seminar it is the analyst who decides what are the relevant topics for discussion, and it is he who decides when to steer the discussion from one topic to the next – though naturally he will take due account of the feelings of the other participants on these matters.

In practice, the most useful length has been found to be between one day and a week – the optimum being perhaps two or three days.

With less time, events inevitably become 'talks' or 'lectures'; with more, they become 'training courses'. Within these limits the approach is informal. The emphasis is on dialogue rather than monologue; on real-life case-study rather than artificial exercise; on joint learning rather than teaching. To this end, numbers of participants are deliberately restricted. Practice has indicated an optimum of about 12–15 people for conference events of several days' length or more. However, larger groups of up to 20 or 30 in size seem to be tolerable where a more specific topic is broached in shorter events.

The actual programme will vary according to the exact purpose of the event. More broadly focused events may start with some formal presentation of general organizational concepts or theories, by the social analyst. Project-linked conferences by contrast, may start with little more than a reminder of the changes in hand or forthcoming, then turn immediately to discuss present or foreseen problems. In general, any conference will include some appropriate mixture of three ingredients: analysis of specific situations and problems experienced by the participants; attempts at conceptual clarification; and discussion of general organizational and procedural 'models'. In other words, though the settings of project work and conference work are decisively different, the actual content of discussion has exactly the same composition in both cases.

## The Establishment of Steering Committees

Where social-analytic activity is directed to first or isolated projects, preparatory discussions of the kind described at the start of the chapter are sufficient to confirm the need for the specific project in mind, and the existence of specific sanction to proceed. But where a more extended relationship is envisaged, either from the very start or as a result of accumulating experience of beneficial collaboration on a series of more limited projects, then the possibility arises of establishing some permanent steering group or committee. Potentially, such a body can serve a number of purposes. First it provides a definite point to which any proposals for new projects, from whatever source, may be directed. Secondly, it provides a definite body to discuss the feasibility and priority of these proposals. Thirdly, it offers a definite place to which the general results of project work may be reported. Fourthly, it provides a place in which the general strategy of the collaboration may be discussed, and also such specific matters as clearance of material for publication, or the design of conference programmes to support specific project work.

Finally, at the point where the social-analytic undertaking as a whole is financed, the steering committee offers a means of systematic appraisal of the success and usefulness of the work, and a place where consideration can be given to extension of finance. Indeed, where finance is to be made available over any extended period of time, some such steering arrangement is essential.

In effect, a specifically constituted steering committee creates an additional level of sanctioning. Before discussions can start with any individual, his own personal sanction is needed. Before discussions can start in any given group, the sanction of the group as a whole is needed. A steering committee allows the possibility of testing the general sanction of the whole social entity concerned, whatever it may be, for the continuance of social-analytic activity.

In the Glacier Project a special Project Steering Committee was formed by the Works Council, as described in Chapter 1. This included both management members and elected representatives of various groups of shop-floor staff. Following this example, several client organizations in the later social welfare projects were encouraged to form similar widely based steering committees, with elected members from various kinds and levels of staff. There was an additional motive for prompting such action. This was to try and avoid the bias that resulted from the tendency to work only on projects identified by senior management groups, with the danger of being seen by others in the same departments simply as 'management men'. The idea was that, as in the Glacier Project, staff at any level would feel free to come forward with problems as they themselves perceived them.

In each case however, these artificially created bodies failed to establish any effective role. The reason for this appears in retrospect to be as follows. The Glacier steering arrangements worked because a mechanism for sanctioning important action and change of all kinds in the Company – not just social-analytic project work – already existed in the shape of the Works Council. This institution itself had taken many years to develop and become effectively established. By contrast, what was being attempted in these other cases was to bring into immediate being a major new institution, with radical implications for the whole approach to management and participation. In effect, what was being attempted was not only the instant creation of a major new piece of organizational structure, but an instant change in the whole underlying culture.

Out of this, a general principle can perhaps be drawn. It seems that steering and sanctioning mechanisms for social-analytic project work can be no more elaborate or broadly based than the present stage of institutional development of the social entity concerned readily allows. Thus, in some particular situation of hierarchic organization, the most realistic steering mechanism may be no more complex than discussions with the chief or head himself. In other similar situations, the obvious steering group will be the head and his immediate associates. In early hospital projects at Brunel, it was natural for work to be guided by a group consisting of the chief administrator, chief nurse, a senior medical representative, and sometimes the treasurer. (Significantly, the key management groups in the new re-organized health service are of similar composition – a coalition of chief officers and clinical representatives.) In other words social analysis must take social institutions, even those needed for its own work, as it finds them in the first instance, and proceed from there. As has already been stressed, one of the essentials in social-analytic work in practice is 'staying with the actors', at whatever stage in the journey they may be.

# PART III

# Broader Issues

# 8 The Scientific Products of Social Analysis

In this third part, we turn away from practice to broader issues – to questions of the evaluation of any changes which may arise from social-analytic work; to questions of the validation of the scientific ideas employed; to examination of the broader values and beliefs which underlie social analysis and the special skills which its practice calls for; and to consideration of the scope for a more extended use of social analysis.

First of all however in this chapter something more must be said about the scientific nature of social analysis. The whole point and purpose of social analysis is to accumulate scientific knowledge, knowledge of a sort that is immediately usable. Now it is no part of the object of this book to attempt any comprehensive statement or summary of all the knowledge and theory about social institutions which has grown out of social-analytic work over the years. Such material is described in detail in various other publications (*see* Appendix B). What is in keeping, however, with a study of the general nature of social analysis, is some discussion of the various different *kinds* of knowledge and theories that have developed, and in what particular way each can be said to be 'scientific'. This we shall now attempt.

We shall see that three broad kinds or layers of scientific material have accumulated. The first is a series of detailed case-studies about work in particular projects and settings. The second layer comprises a variety of scientific generalizations about social institutions which have developed out of individual projects. These are in the shape of 'requisite models' which can be widely employed to facilitate design and change. The third is a deeper layer of social theory about man in organized society, which has also gradually formed as project work has proceeded and specific institutional models have accrued. Thus, the material in each layer is intimately related to that of the other two. In social-analytic work, 'empirical research' and 'theory development' go hand in hand in a way which is, to say the least, unusual in social science.

## The Accumulation of Case-Study Material

As has already been discussed, the nature of social-analytic exploration, geared as it is to the deeper and more ambiguous aspects of social institutions, is not one that generates much empirical material in the shape of straightforward measurements or statistics. There is no body of systematic records or observations to which one may turn in social analysis and say – here is the basic data. As written material accumulates in any project, first in the form of the analyst's own rough working notes, and then in the form of agreed reports, it already contains a rich mixture, including perhaps selected quotations of the manifest situation taken from official documents, statements of various actors' different working assumptions, notes of other relevant features of the working situation, and strivings towards more requisite formulations. (*See* the various specimen project reports in Appendix A.) Since social institutions when examined at any depth can rarely be discovered to exist in sharp and unquestioned form, there is no firm boundary between the 'is' and the 'ought', the 'existent' and the 'becoming' – which again is precisely why a collaborative, exploratory method is more appropriate than a forced attempt at 'objective' study.

At the empirical level then, the main product of social-analytic activity comes in the form of various specific descriptions of the excavations as it were, undertaken in particular organizational settings, and the material unearthed or refined *en route*. A wealth of case-study material of this kind has in fact been published in respect of the Glacier Metal Project, a variety of projects in health services, and a variety of projects in the social welfare field (*see* Appendix B).

However, as was noted in Chapter 4, the production of straightforward factual descriptions of certain aspects of social institutions is not impossible in principle, even though it may be limited in scope, nor is the provision of other factual data which may bear on certain aspects of institutional design. Accordingly, in addition to specific reports of various exploratory projects of the kind just described, there exists as well a certain amount of factual survey material which has been gathered in the course of, or independently of, collaborative exploration. For example, a number of factual surveys of the earning-progressions of·individuals throughout their working careers have been undertaken. There have also been a number of factual surveys of the 'time-spans of discretion' inherent in a wide variety of jobs in industrial and other settings, and of associated expressions of 'felt-fair pay' by their holders.[1]

## 'Requisite Models'

The initial scientific product of social analysis comes in the form, then, of a series of detailed reports of case-studies in social-analytic exploration (with some associated surveys), including much material of highly specific nature. It would be generally agreed, however, that the straightforward accumulation of empirical material does not by itself constitute a thorough-going scientific approach. What has social analysis to reveal by way of genuine scientific generalizations?

Before this question can be answered some clarification of the essential nature of scientific propositions in the social sciences has to be undertaken. The idea of what will be called the *requisite model* has to be established, and distinguished from the more familiar one of the *causal law*. This particular distinction turns out in fact to be closely related to the one already established in previous chapters, the distinction between two fundamentally different approaches to social study or social intervention: an 'action' approach and a 'behavioural' approach.

It will be remembered that in an 'action' approach to study or change, man is seen as a being imbued with his own aims and values, constructing his own definitions of the meanings of any situation in which he finds himself, and in consequence needing to make his own choices about which way he goes. By contrast in 'behavioural' approaches, it is only the viewpoint of the observer or interventionist which is allowed validity. Any activity or statement on the part of the 'subject' is seen as so much 'behaviour', the significance of which is to be determined and evaluated by the observer himself.

Within a behavioural approach there is no obvious difficulty or contradiction in employing the sort of causal law or hypothesis found in the natural sciences. This is a statement of the form 'the occur-

[1] For a comprehensive review of the work here, with detailed references to the original sources, *see* Jaques (1976), *A General Theory of Bureaucracy*, pp. 162–5, 228–31.

rence of events Y *cause* in certain given circumstances effects X [2] because of . . . (here reference to some deeper explanatory theory)'.[3] For example, 'bringing a flame to a mixture of sulphur, saltpetre and carbon (Y) *causes* in dry conditions an explosion (X), because of . . . . (here reference to chemical theory)'.

Causal statements or hypotheses of this kind may be readily transformed into what may be called *technological* statements, that is statements of the kind 'given desired results and circumstances X, action Y is necessary'.[4] For example, 'given the desired result of an explosion and dry circumstances (X), the action (Y) of bringing a flame to a mixture of sulphur, saltpetre and carbon is necessary'.

However, the problems of establishing such causal propositions or technological prescriptions, in what we have just described as 'action' approaches, are immediately apparent. What happens when the various constituent elements of the situation, unlike molecules of sulphur or carbon, make up their own minds as to how they are going to respond to given situational change? How can notions of cause and determined effect be incorporated into an approach which has ideas of choice and uncertainty at its very centre? How is it possible, on the one hand, to talk about freely choosing actors, and on the other, to talk about predicting with scientific certainty what the outcomes of their choices must be?[5] Moreover, it is clear, as we have said before, that social analysis implies an action approach. The idea of men as actors, constructing their own interpretation of life and making their own decisions, pervades everything that is done. Indeed, the very idea of a 'social institution' is itself firmly rooted in an action view. Concepts such as 'stimulus', 'response' or

[2] The reason for the apparent oddity of putting a 'Y' *before* an 'X' will become clearer when in the transformation to a technological form to be undertaken below, the X-term takes its natural place as the 'given', and the Y-term as that which 'follows'.

[3] Full scientific explanation does not simply involve statements of regularity or correlation, but always invokes some deeper theory, some underlying models, some new ways of representing things. Moreover, such explanations can never purport to have universal applicability, but only to be valid in, or in the absence of, certain given circumstances. *See* Toulmin (1953), *The Philosophy of Science.*

[4] It may be noted that any scientific proposition can be changed into what may be described as a technological one, merely by a shift of grammatical form as it were, in which the *predicted* outcomes are elevated to the status of *desired* outcomes.

[5] This problem is not new to those writers who recognize the possibility of a distinctive 'action' approach to human questions. *See*, for example, Winch (1958), *The Idea of a Social Science*, pp. 92–3; Emmett (1966), *Rules, Roles and Relations*, pp. 109–27; Simey (1968), *Social Science and Social Purpose*, p. 166; Szasz (1974), *Ideology and Insanity*, p. 199.

'habit' may exist happily in a behavioural world, but that of a 'social institution' sits very oddly indeed.

The way out of the impasse has to be the recognition of a quite different kind of scientific proposition. It is one that may usefully be distinguished by the adjective 'requisite' rather than 'causal'. Although the idea of causality has to be abandoned, the more fundamental scientific notion of the possibility of hypothesis and test need not be however. This second kind of scientific proposition takes the general form 'social arrangements Y *are consistent* with given needs and circumstances X, because of . . . (here reference to some deeper explanatory theory)'. In its technological version, where it can readily be described as a *requisite model*, it will take the more straightforward form 'given needs and circumstances X, social arrangements Y are requisite'.

Thus a proposition that the action of adopting or enacting a particular social arrangement Y is requisite given particular needs and circumstances X, does not attempt to predict how people will actually act if this is done, or whether or not, therefore, the given needs will be met on any single occasion. What it does predict, is that no contradictions will be revealed between the social arrangement adopted, and the conditions which it has been expressly brought into being to meet. It proposes that certain arrangements will generally prove to be workable in practice: that they will help rather than hinder the people who are using them in the given circumstances to achieve their desired ends. As such the requisite proposition is still (like the causal law) testable; it is still *falsifiable*.[6] Practice may reveal that inconsistencies do indeed exist in principle so that the proposition needs to be scrapped or modified. The test, therefore, is not just one of internal or logical coherence (though this

[6] The reference here is of course to Karl Popper's idea of scientific propositions not as statements which can ever finally be demonstrated as 'true', but essentially as generalized conjectures, gradually gaining force as successive experience fails to refute them (Popper, 1974, *Conjectures and Refutations*). Whether a 'requisite model' is equivalent to the sociological notion of an 'ideal type' is an interesting question. Weber tends to treat the 'ideal type' as a pattern of purely rational action, never actually achieved in practice (Weber, 1964, *The Theory of Social and Economic Organization*). By contrast, a 'requisite model' might be said to be fully achievable in practice, at least in the situation where it was adopted by enactment, and where there was a large measure of consensus that this was now the prevailing social institution (which is of course a different thing from saying that all observable *behaviour* would necessarily adhere to it). On the other hand, Schutz' conception of the ideal type as the means by which we comprehend all indirect social experience would certainly seem to have interesting similarities to the notion of requisite model (Schutz, 1972, *The Phenomenology of the Social World*).

may be part of it), but one against actual social reality as it is lived and experienced.

Like the causal law, the requisite model is a general proposition of an 'if . . . . then' form. '*If* certain circumstances and needs X are given . . . ., *then* arrangements Y are appropriate, suitable, requisite.' Requisite models are not simple injunctions. They are not simple prescriptions of what 'ought' to be done. If the 'if' part of the proposition (that is, any of the circumstances or needs to be taken as 'givens') is changed for any reason, then the 'then' part of the proposition (that is, what is requisite) necessarily alters as well.

## Examples of Requisite Models – The Model of the Managerial Role

Let us consider a number of actual examples derived from social-analytic work in order to illustrate this idea of the requisite proposition, or requisite model. We will take for a start the conception of the managerial role which grew in the first instance out of work in the Glacier Project.[7] The initial statement of the problem could be said, in effect, to be this: what minimal authority (Y) is appropriately allocated to somebody called a 'manager', if the condition (X) is set that he can reasonably be held accountable for the work of his subordinates? Given the circumstances and conditions of the industrial setting at Glacier Metal (typical no doubt of a much wider range) the general answer was that a manager must have, at minimum, authority of veto in the selection of people who were actually to be subordinate to him, authority to remove inadequate people from such a position, authority to assess them and assign suitable work to them, and authority to 'differentially reward', that is, to decide what share of any available pay increases each should have. This proposition is testable in principle and indeed was thoroughly tested in practice in Glacier Metal. As it transpired in practice, one of the additional conditions necessary was the existence of an effective system to allow the individual to appeal against the decision of his manager, should he feel that the latter was misusing his authority (*see* below).

In moving from the field of private industry to public services, however, exploration revealed difficulties with this precise formulation. It rapidly became apparent, for example, that it could not be taken as unquestioned in this new setting that 'managers' would or should have the right to make decisions about the appropriate size

[7] See *Exploration in Management*, Chapter 4.

and timing of individual pay increases for their subordinates. By and large, the cultural norm in the public service field included a general expectation that employees during their careers should experience regular progression in predetermined steps through some given pay grade or grades. Nor, given the prevailing expectations of secure employment in this same field would it be requisite to talk directly of the right of a manager to remove inadequate subordinates from posts subordinate to him.

With this change in the needs and conditions (X) to be taken into account, a change in arrangements (Y) would necessarily follow. Instead of authority to 'differentially reward', a more appropriate statement of authority for managers in the public setting would be that of the right to make official appraisals which might affect future career opportunities. And instead of authority to remove from post, the requisite could be no stronger than authority to initiate possible transfer, by submitting official reports of the assessed unsuitability of the person concerned for his present position.[8]

This example illustrates sharply the point already made that requisite statements are not simply prescriptions or injunctions, but more complex propositions of an 'if . . . . then' form. If (as here) the 'if' part of the proposition is changed, then the 'then' part of the proposition necessarily alters as well.

### Examples of More Complex Requisite Models – Two Models for the Organization of Medical Work

Let us consider now some more complex requisite models. The particular examples to be looked at build at various points on the *managerial* role model which we have just discussed, and the *co-ordinating* and *monitoring* role models described in the case-study of the senior hospital officers in Chapter 2.

The first example concerns the way in which the work of doctors in hospitals may be organized. Here, the existence of two contrasted models became apparent very early in social-analytic work in the health services. The first, which may be described as the 'agency service' pattern was the type which had tended to predominate in the old publicly owned hospitals of the late nineteenth and early twentieth century – the fever hospitals, sanatoria and mental hospitals. The other, which might be described as the 'independent medical practitioner' pattern, had predominated in the old voluntary and teaching hospitals. (In some of the hospitals explored in

---

[8] See *Hospital Organization*, pp. 42–5, and *Social Services Departments*, p. 261.

social-analytic project work in the late 1960s, a degree of uncertainty and confusion was evident as to which of these two applied, particularly in those ex-local-authority hospitals which still retained posts with titles such as 'medical superintendent' or 'medical administrator'.) The different organizational forms implicit in these two models are illustrated in Figure 8.1. In the 'agency' model there is one clear boss at the top. He is accountable not only for the general administration of all the medical staff, but also for the clinical or technical quality of their work. The system is built on a hierarchy of managerial relationships, and all the medical staff are in effect 'assistants' to the head doctor (Medical Superintendent or Chief Medical Officer). Since this head is himself the 'officer' of some appointing authority, patients are in effect receiving service identifiable with the employing authority itself (the 'Health Committee' the 'Hospital Board') and it will be a matter of some chance as to which doctor actually administers it.

By sharp contrast, patients in the other model will identify the service strongly with the individual specialist or consultant in whose hands they find themselves. They are not patients of the such-and-such health authority: they are patients of Doctor A. Now this specialist or consultant may have his own 'juniors' (that is, registrars or house-officers) who are clearly subordinate to him, and who may in fact carry the bulk of the immediate contact with the patient. But Dr A himself will recognize no higher 'boss', 'director' or 'manager'. Within certain understood limits of custom, law, professional ethics and employment contract, he has indeed complete freedom. He has, that is, genuine 'clinical autonomy' to exercise his believed expertise in treating the patient (given the consent of the latter) exactly as he thinks best. In practice, his work will be subject to *monitoring* for adherence to the limits just mentioned, and will be *co-ordinated* with the work of other doctors and other health service professionals in various ways. However, in no precise sense of the word will his own work be *managed*.[9]

Now from the social analyst's view it must again be stressed that neither of these models is obviously 'good' or 'bad'. What he is primarily concerned to do is to establish the relationships of each to various possible criteria so as to understand better, and to help those with whom he works to understand better, which situations call for one model and which for the other.

[9] For further discussion of these issues see *Hospital Organization*, Chapter 5; also Brunel Institute of Organization and Social Studies (1976b), *Professionals in Health and Social Services Organizations,*

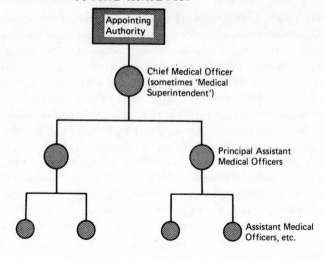

(a) 'Agency' medical services — extended hierarchy

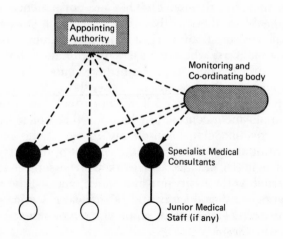

(b) Independent medical practitioners — collegial organization

*Figure 8.1    Two Alternative Models of Medical Organization*

The first model, agency medical service, provides for focused accountability, but by the same token it implies that a chief can be
found who could realistically be held accountable for the totality of
work of his subordinate staff. It implies, that is, a relatively narrow

spread of medical technologies, or put another way, a relatively small development in medical specialities. It provides for strong control and co-ordination, but it implies the willingness of patients to accept an agency type of service. By contrast, the second model, independent medical practice, allows a wide development of medical specialities. Moreover, it is consonant with a particular cultural assumption that the thing of prime importance in medicine is the establishment of a direct personal link between the patient and his physician, a relationship of choice and trust which must be stronger than any other relationship which binds the latter. At the same time there is less ready control of the situation by external parties. It is a system which makes it more difficult for example for the employing authority or its officers to introduce new policies about the allocation of time and attention to particular kinds of cases should they think it right to do so. It makes it more difficult to hasten the widespread adoption of new (and believed to be better) clinical methods or procedures. Thus, depending on which of these various sets of needs (X) are given prominence, one or the other of these two organizational forms (Y) will be more suitable. And again, if either organizational form (Y) turns out in practice to be inconsistent with the full range of relevant criteria (X) exposed by experience, then it will need to be modified.

## A Second Example of Complex Models – Hospital Social Work

As a second example of more complex modelling, let us consider the present situation with regard to the provision of social work in hospitals in England and Wales. This reveals an even wider variety of possibilities (Y) depending on which of a range of possible criteria (X) are given predominance.[10] In the major reorganizations of 1974 it was decreed that responsibility for provision of social work in hospitals, formerly lying with health authorities, should now be passed to the Social Services Departments of local authorities. This meant that hospital social workers would now become fellow-employees of the child care officers, welfare officers, mental health officers and other social workers who had already been incorporated into these Departments at the time of their formation several years before. The question was, how could social work services in hospitals now best be provided?

Analysis revealed at least three basic models (Figure 8.2). At the

10 *See* Hey and Rowbottom (1974).

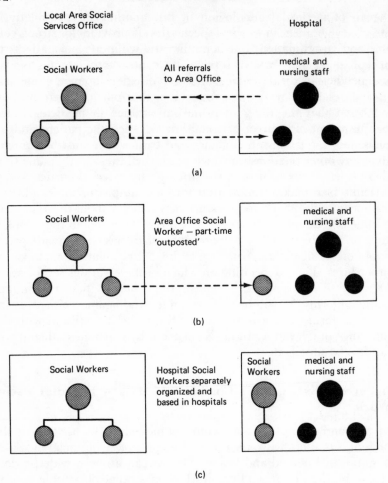

Figure 8.2    Three Models of Provision of Hospital Social Work

extreme, all hospital social workers could be completely amal-
gamated into the existing local area social services offices. Where
patients needed social work support, hospital staff could refer
directly to the Area Office. There the case might be allocated to
any social worker who was available (Figure 8.2a). Alternatively, one
or more social workers from the Area Office might be outposted to
work in the hospital itself during certain set sessions, during which
time they would pick up work on all outstanding cases, though still
clearly regarded as part of the staff of the Office and accountable to

the Area Officer in charge (Figure 8.2b). As a further possibility, the situation might be left much as inherited, with certain social workers working permanently in hospitals, and separately organized under a principal hospital social worker, though now as members of the Social Services Department, therefore ultimately responsible to, and the responsibility of, the Director of Social Services (Figure 8.2c).

What also emerged from project work was the wide range of circumstances and needs (X) which had to be taken into account in evaluating the suitability of one model rather than another for any given situation, for example:

(1) the proximity of the hospital and the corresponding Area Social Services Office;
(2) the total volume of social work generated by the hospital, and the catchment area from which cases were drawn;
(3) the desirability of building close and continuing personal links between the social workers involved in any case on the one hand, and doctors and nurses on the other;
(4) the need for continuity of social work for patients leaving hospital and returning home;
(5) the need to provide career opportunities to allow staff both to develop specialized skills and (where capable) to progress to higher organizational levels.

Various choices (Y) would become requisite depending on the relative weight given to these various criteria (X). Thus Model (a) is facilitated by the close proximity of hospital and Area Offices; Model (b) acknowledges a less than full-time workload; Model (c) promotes close liaison with medical and nursing staff; and so forth.

## Models for Perquisites and Procedure

In all the models described so far, the propositions of requisite action (Y) have either been about the functions, authority or accountability to be assigned to those in some particular position in an organized group (what would often be referred to in one usage of the word as requisite 'roles'), or alternatively about the structure and composition of some larger system (what would often be referred to in one usage as requisite 'organization'). However, as was noted in Chapter 3, the meat or material of enactable institutions is not limited only to statements of functions, authority and accountability, or to statements of structure and composition. It may also include statements of the perquisites and rewards attached to particular positions, and statements of general rules or procedures for regulating social interaction. And indeed models embodying both these further elements have in fact arisen in social-analytic practice.

In the Glacier Project various questions of pay and status were explored. Model payment and progression systems (Y) were developed in terms of criteria (X) such as the need to reward higher responsibility with higher pay; the need to have regular reviews of individual pay in the light of individual development and performance; and the need to have regular reviews of general pay level in the light of economic inflation.[11]

In another part of the same project the handling of individual grievances was analysed. A detailed appeals procedure was negotiated, published within the Company Policy Document and put into general use. This applied to any situation where a member of the Company was dissatisfied with any decision of his manager which affected him and which he believed to be unfair or unjust. It dealt for example with such things as who was to hear appeals in the first place; how the appellant might be represented at hearings if he wished; what was to happen if the appellant failed to turn up; and what was to happen if he, or the manager-appealed-against, wished to take matters to a higher level still.[12]

Again, it is readily possible to extract the criteria (X) against which this procedure (Y) must be judged. They include an assumption that it is impossible in the nature of things to devise or negotiate general rules or policies which will satisfactorily cover every case which subsequently arises. They include also an assumption that where the application of a general rule or policy in a particular case rests on the judgement of an individual manager, then the possibility in principle of error or partiality must always follow. Overall, of course, there is an assumption that equity and justice are in themselves desirable things. In the end then, the model rests on certain cultural or value assumptions. Were, for example, the question to arise of using this particular model in a radically different cultural setting, then no doubt a careful reconsideration of its validity would be necessary.

[11] *See* Jaques (1967), *Equitable Payment*, Appendix 2. It should be emphasized perhaps that these various models have not always been *expounded* in the form of proposition of the kind 'if X . . . ., then Y . . . .'. The point is however that it is in every case readily possible to recast the original statement in this form.

[12] See *Exploration in Management*, Chapter 18.

## Criteria of Requisiteness

As will be seen from the various examples that have now been examined, any of an extremely diverse range of needs and circumstances may be germane to the choice of institutional models. Some, of course, will be wholly particular to given social settings and are not of general scientific significance – the fortuitous combination of personalities and abilities in a given situation, local geography, specific limitations on accommodation or finance, and the like.

Of more general requirements, we have just considered the frequently experienced need to maintain clear lines of individual accountability, albeit coupled with right of appeal against managerial authority. We have noted the desire in many situations of professional practice to maintain the paramount strength of the personal relationship with the client or patient, or to build at all costs close and continuing personal links between the various professional workers who find themselves involved in the same cases. We have seen in some situations the pressing requirement to observe the reality of the physical separation of various co-workers; or the need to take due account of continuing shortages of human or other resources. To these we might add a host of others: needs to observe particular work requirements, such as the provision of a continuous 24-hour nursing service in hospitals, or say the introduction of some new automated process in industry; needs for reasonable career prospects for employees; needs to provide work which matches a wide range of different and changing abilities and interests; needs to build teams and work-groups which encourage participation and enrich the quality of social life of people at work; and so on.

It would appear then, that the needs and conditions which determine requisite institutions, the criteria against which institutions offered as requisite must be judged, are of the widest possible variety: social, psychological, technical, economic and so on. It would seem to follow clearly enough that there is no 'one best' organizational form. All is relative. Almost any conceivable variety of institutional arrangements might turn out to have some utility, depending on the particular range of needs and conditions which prevail.[13]

[13] This might be said to be the viewpoint adopted in the 'contingency theory' of organization, often associated with Lawrence and Lorsch (1967), *Organization and Environment*, but stemming from a broader school including the work of Burns and Stalker (1961); Woodward (1965); Pugh, Hickson and associates (1963, 1968, 1969) and some of the later Tavistock work on 'socio-technical' design as in Herbst (1974). However, some of these writers extend the idea even further. In seeking to establish

However this is not the only way to view the matter. Elliott Jaques has suggested that all requisite organization (and his use of 'requisite' here is clearly much stronger than simply 'appropriate' or 'contingent') must satisfy two major and universal criteria. The first is that the institutional arrangements concerned must help to produce outputs or products of real social value; in other words that they help to get good work done. The second is that the institutions concerned are not in his phrase 'paranoiagenic'. That is, all things being equal, the institutions should help to reduce aggression, envy and paranoid anxiety, and help to promote trust and confidence amongst the various individuals and groups who act or work within them. Taking it to a higher level of generality still, he suggests that the ultimate test of the requisite institution is its ability or otherwise to forward the survival of the race.[14] From this point of view then, models of requisite organization are not just elaborate chains of contingency, but statements which carry some element of universal or absolute force.

Here then are two significantly different views of the meaning of 'requisiteness'. Earlier in the chapter we have stressed the relative nature of requisite models. Would the adoption of this second view negate all that we have said? In fact it would not, although some major shift or extension in approach would certainly follow. Even with a less resolutely relativist or pragmatic stance, it is still possible to cast requisite models in the form of 'if . . . . . then . . . . . .' propositions; propositions capable of being tested, and falsified or confirmed, by experience. In other words, the social analyst is still able to stick resolutely to a scientific approach. However, given this second stance, the analyst is now no longer obliged to take whatever statements of needs those with whom he is working choose to make, at face value, and without comment or criticism. He may feel free to question whether the particular 'ifs' adopted are themselves consistent with broader or more general 'ifs' or needs, such as, say, the value of promoting more widespread participation in the control of

---

statistical correlations between various organizational forms on the one hand, and the given conditions and circumstances in which they arise on the other, they seem to imply that there is some *causal* link between the two. Such a view, of course, as we have just observed, leaves no scope for free-choosing human actors or indeed for any theory of deliberate institutional design. Criticisms of this determinist approach to organizational studies have been expounded in Silverman (1970), *The Theory of Organizations*; and Child (1972), 'Organizational Structure, Environment and the Role of Strategic Choice'.

[14] *See* Jaques (1976), *A General Theory of Bureaucracy*. In his own description requisite institutions are those which are 'called for by the nature of things, including man's nature' (p. 6).

major social enterprises, or the general desirability of building a climate of greater social trust. Indeed there may be certain very basic values to which the social analyst himself, as a matter of profound personal conviction, would wish to adhere at all costs – an issue which we will explore more thoroughly in Chapter 10.

Such discussion leads us beyond consideration of specific institutional models to the third and deeper layer of theories and ideas which have developed from social-analytic work over the years, mentioned at the start of the chapter.

## The Development of Deeper Social Ideas and Theories

Before proceeding to this deeper layer however, let us briefly review the ground we have covered so far. It is, as has been said, quite beyond the scope of this book to provide a comprehensive or exhaustive description of all the models that have actually been developed in social-analytic work, or the needs or conditions to which they have been shown to relate. The purpose of looking at the specific models described has been simply to reinforce and exemplify the general ideas expressed earlier. To recapitulate: the scientific product of social-analytic work is not simply an empirical record or case-study of many specific problem situations explored. Scientific propositions of a truly general and testable form emerge as well. But arising as they do from an 'action' view of man, they take the distinctive form of the 'requisite proposition' or the 'requisite model', in contrast to the more familiar 'causal law' to be encountered in 'behavioural' approaches to social studies and in the biological and physical sciences.

However, no truly developed science stops short at this point either. In its testable propositions, whatever precise form they take, there will always be reference to some more general theory which attempts to explain just why these particular propositions come to be true. Underneath the middle-level generalizations and propositions will be found a number of deeper-level ideas and conceptions which are not in themselves testable, or at least so directly testable. Often these deeper ideas will act as a seed-bed from which various directly testable hypotheses grow. At the same time they themselves will undergo more or less gradual change as further empirical experience accumulates. These deeper ideas may be variously referred to as axioms, the fundamental assumptions or (insofar as they communicate a picture of how scientific endeavour in the field in question should proceed) the paradigms. In the social sciences, certain basic values or ideologies will inevitably be found to be embedded within them.

Within social analysis, in addition to the variety of requisite models described, there has developed over the years a rich substratum of such fundamental theory. Moreover, much of it can be readily related to other established ideas in sociology, psychology, law and political philosophy.

There is for example the powerfully interlocking nexus of general theories, developed by Elliott Jaques out of his Glacier work in the first instance, on the important social topics of levels of responsibility within work, equitable payment for different levels of work, rates of individual progression within working life, and the fit or misfit of individual capacities to 'size' of job.[15] The whole is centred on a conception of the nature of all human work in organized settings as involving the exercise of greater or lesser degrees of discretion, within prescribed limits, and towards more or less chronologically distant prescribed ends. In later expositions of these theories, explicit reference is made to the phenomenological writings of such people as Bergson, Dewey and Schutz.[16] From this central idea extend two separate lines of further consideration. One pursues the nature of work considered as a psychological phenomenon; that is, work as it is subjectively experienced and coped with by the individual. Here questions arise of differences between individuals in their capacities to exercise choice and to withstand the anxiety of uncertainty in the pursuit of deferred ends. Links are made here with psychoanalytic ideas. The second pursues the nature of work as a social phenomenon, in terms of the prescribed limitations and ends imposed in various social circumstances.

Following the first line Jaques himself has developed a bold hypothesis about the existence of certain basic discontinuities in human capacity, and has attempted to identify in broad terms the qualitative differences involved.[17] Following the second line, an equally fundamental corresponding theory has been developed. This postulates the existence of a natural hierarchy of discrete and qualitatively different levels of work to be carried out within human organizations, and explores the implications for organizational design.[18]

[15] See Jaques (1956, 1965a, 1965b, 1967, 1970, 1976).

[16] See Jaques (1976), op. cit., Part III.

[17] Jaques (1965a), 'Speculations Concerning Level of Capacity', and Jaques (1976), op. cit., Chapter 9.

[18] Rowbottom and Billis (1977), 'The Stratification of Work and Organizational Design'.

As observed earlier, there has been considerable concentration in social analysis on the detailed and fundamental analysis of the nature of social roles: what the very word 'role' means; what various kinds of obligations (duties) and rights (authority) can be found in particular roles; how roles become institutionalized; and how institutionalized roles interact with the more ephemeral ones into which people slip hour by hour in the course of their normal social life. Again, explicit linkages have been traced to various formative sociological and psychological ideas in this field.[19]

In pursuing general questions of managerial authority and participation in modern society, Brown and Jaques have both advanced important ideas on the nature of social authority and social power and the proper relationships between them. Legislative, executive and appeals processes in organizations have been separated in concept, and the different institutional requirements of each have been analysed. The rights of all employees in a just and democratic society to participate in the control of their own enterprises, to legitimate the areas of authority of their managers and to appeal against believed misuses of such authority, have been explored.[20] Here the discussion has inevitably touched on many of the perennial issues of political philosophy such as the fundamental nature of authority, government, law and justice.

In another area attention has turned to the basic nature and characteristics of professional groups in modern society, in the attempt to throw light on such general questions as the meaning of 'professional independence', how far professionals can properly be managed in their work, the practical significance of differences in status and authority amongst the professions, and the like.[21] Here again, the exploration moves on to well-trodden ground in sociological theory and research.

Finally, one might draw attention to the attempt in social-analytic theory to explore and make explicit its own methodology and its relation to other kinds of social research and social intervention, of which of course this book itself is a part.

It is impossible to offer here more than the sketchiest outlines of most of these ideas, and any who are interested to know more of them and their relation to other or broader social theories will have

[19] Jaques (1976), op. cit., Chapters 2 and 17.
[20] Brown (1960), *Exploration in Management*; Brown (1971), Organization; Brown (1973), *The Earnings Conflict*; Jaques (1976), op. cit.
[21] Brunel Institute of Organization and Social Studies (1976b), *Professionals in Health and Social Services Organization, A Working Paper*.

to consult the sources referred to. However, what must be emphasized again is that none of the specific theories at even this fundamental level have grown in isolation. All have sprung in the first instance from analysis within, and reflection upon, specific pieces of project-work, however this may have been fertilized by other established ideas in the social and political sciences. The general theory of the work-pay-capacity nexus, for instance, grew out of a request for help in a specific job evaluation problem facing a small group of clerical staff at Glacier Metal.[22] The descriptive theory of organizational work strata sprang from observations accumulated in the course of social-analytic work in a small number of Social Services Departments.[23]

Moreover these general theories, as they have gradually developed, have powerfully influenced later project-work. As pointed out earlier, there can be no question that the social analyst in some way off-loads all previous conceptions before he commences exploration of some new project area, or indeed that he ought to do so. On the contrary, he now comes into new discussion relatively richly equipped with already formed intellectual tools – though always ready to abandon or reshape them should experience indicate the necessity to do so. The isolation of the activity which is conventionally described as 'developing social theory' from 'carrying out empirical research' is one which is completely foreign to the social analyst.[24] Because his work is always concerned with attempting to discover those scientific generalizations which will provide the key to effective action in situations of immediate social problems, the making of hypothesis and the carrying out of empirical tests are seen as activities to be pursued side by side, within the same arena. Theorizing, empirical study, and problem-solving, are seen as a trio, which have everything to gain by proceeding hand in hand, and everything to lose by separation.

[22] Jaques (1956), *Measurement of Responsibility*, Chapter 2.

[23] Rowbottom and Billis (1976), op. cit.

[24] Many writers have expressed concern with the evident gap in existing social sciences between broad theory and empirical research. There is for example Merton's plea for more 'theories of the middle range' (Merton, 1968, *Social Theory and Social Structure*); also Wright Mills' castigation of implicitly conservative 'grand theorizing' on the one hand, and the triviality of much 'abstracted empiricism' on the other (Mills, 1970, *The Sociological Imagination*). *See* however Dahrendorf's criticism of some of these analyses. In his essays 'Out of Utopia' (Dahrendorf, 1968c) and 'Sociology and the Sociologist' (Dahrendorf, 1968e), he argues, as we do here, that the divide between social theory and social research can only be healed if social scientists shift their concentration from 'questions' to 'problems'. (The Dahrendorf quotation reproduced at the start of the book is from the second essay just mentioned.)

# 9 Evaluation and Validation

It is part of the scientific tenor of our times to insist increasingly that no large-scale programme of social innovation or development – be it the widespread introduction of a new drug or a new teaching method, or a new approach to community development, or a new form of management training – is undertaken without some explicit accompaniment of systematic evaluation. In keeping with this out-look it is quite proper to enquire what happens about evaluation in social-analytic work. Putting it more crudely, it may be asked (and often has been asked): what evidence is there that social analysis actually pays off?

The trouble of course with simple questions is that they often fail to take note of real complexities. In attempting to assess the general value of social-analytic work there are in fact four specific and some-what separate issues to be considered.

(1) What increased knowledge of social institutions has accrued as a result of social analysis?
(2) How do we know that it is scientifically valid?
(3) How and where has it demonstrated its usefulness by influenc-ing actual enacted change?
(4) How do we know that any such change is in any case beneficial?

As far as the first issue is concerned we have already in the previous chapter looked generally at the kind of knowledge about social institutions that has accrued from social-analytic work, albeit without attempting any comprehensive summary. Moreover, we have tried to demonstrate that this knowledge is of a kind that may properly be described as 'scientific'. Apart from empirical case-study material, there is a whole host of general testable propositions in the form of 'requisite models', and beyond this there is a sizeable ac-cumulation of deeper social theory.

As far as the third issue is concerned – how far this knowledge has demonstrated its applicability in actual enacted change – apart from quoting isolated case-studies, we have been content to refer to a much more detailed and extensive range of reports of particular projects published elsewhere. (However, a brief overview of the present situation in this regard is undertaken in the final chapter.)

The issues to be considered in this chapter then are the fourth and second ones just listed: how any enacted change which occurs as a result of social-analytic work can be evaluated, and (closely associated with this) how the scientific ideas on which it is based can be proved to have general validity. The main concern in this chapter is not with the evaluation of social analysis itself, although we shall in fact return briefly to this topic at a later point.

## The Diffuse Nature of Evaluation in Real-Life Social Change

Let us start with some general consideration of the nature of the evaluation of 'real-life' social change, that is, social change outside an artificially contrived experimental or laboratory setting (leaving aside for the moment the second question of scientific validation). On a first view any process of evaluation might seem a straight-forward enough matter in principle. Certain objectives have been identified; certain actions have been taken; certain results accrue. A comparison (preferably in quantitative terms) between the actual results and the desired objectives will simply determine how success-ful the whole process has been.

Of course it is not as simple as this. Firstly, there are usually no definite and unquestionable 'objectives' all readily identified, pre-defined and agreed in any real-life situation of social change. The start will often be some much more diffuse, ill-formulated feeling of unease or need for change – poor labour relations, a general sense of inadequate coordination or poor organization, a desire for better-focused development work, or whatever it may be. The work of sorting out exactly what objectives should be pursued, and the specific criteria to be used in judging suitable steps towards them, will be a crucial part of the whole process. Secondly, there may well be consequences of any actions eventually taken which are not only unexpected and unintended, but which raise radical questions about the validity or comprehensiveness of the objectives and criteria adopted in the first place; or indeed about the whole initial concep-tion of the nature of the problem. Thirdly, useful quantitative meas-ures may simply not be available. The goals to be pursued and the criteria to be satisfied, may not be things which by their nature can be captured in precise measurements without losing their essence.

Here again we may usefully employ the distinction between 'action' and 'behavioural' approaches established in previous chapters. On the one hand, there is the situation in which the researcher-cum-interventionist feels free to set the rules and objectives himself, and to evaluate what outcomes are relevant and how these match with the criteria he himself has settled upon. This presupposes that he is able to persuade (or coerce) any human subjects involved to play the game according to his rules and to stick to experimental or controlled conditions.

In 'action' approaches none of these things are assumed (and it is in this sense that the phrase 'real-life' is employed here). The human actors concerned will themselves press strongly to join in the processes of fixing the objectives and rules, and of judging the significance of outcomes, both intended or unintended. There is likely to be a more or less continual challenging and revision of general aims and specific criteria, and a more or less perpetual emergence of new problems or new aspects of problems, as action and change proceed.[1]

Which approach is valid will of course vary according to the

---

[1] Marris and Rein provide innumerable examples of the clash of 'action' and 'behavioural' approaches as we distinguish them here, in their comprehensive review of the various large-scale American poverty relief programmes of the 1960s and the attempts to build impartial evaluation into them (Marris and Rein, 1974, *Dilemmas of Social Reform*). By and large, these associated evaluation activities were unsuccessful. Indeed, given the way in which they were framed, they were doomed to failure from the start. 'As the research direction began to specify their needs it became clear that the integrity of an objective evaluation could only be defended by the ruthless subordination of all other claims' (p. 243). 'In practice then, the projects could not realize their claim to be experiments without abandoning their determination to benefit the communities in which they worked. They were not demonstrations but *explorations* of the possibilities of reform' (p. 260, our italics). Nevertheless, established texts on evaluative research continue to stick to straightforward behavioural views. 'Evaluative research refers to those procedures for collecting and analysing data which increase the possibility for "proving" rather than "asserting" the worth of some social activity' (Suchman, 1967, *Evaluation Research*, p. 8. *See also* Caro (1971) *Readings in Evaluation Research*). In a critical review of this field, Westley (1975) distinguishes what he calls 'quantitative-experimental' approaches from 'analytic-inductive' ones (in which he specifically includes social analysis). He suggests that the former, more conventional approaches frequently fail in conditions of 'change, complexity and innovation'. The connection here with 'behavioural' and 'action' approaches is obvious. *See also* similar critical analysis of conventional approaches in various papers by Irwin Deutscher of the Group for Evaluation Research and Programme Improvement, Case Western Reserve University, Ohio.

circumstance. In much biomedical work, or in behaviour-modification programmes such as arise for example in the training of mentally subnormal children, a behavioural approach will be appropriate. Moreover, 'evaluation' will be comparatively unproblematic in principle, and hardly distinguishable from the main research process. It will simply be a matter of establishing by test and observation whether certain actions on the part of the researcher-interventionist produce certain expected results. By contrast, in many kinds of psychotherapy, in social casework, in community development, or in higher education, an 'action' approach will be implicit. Evaluation will be a correspondingly more complex matter which will always necessitate consideration of the views and values of the actors concerned.

## What the Social Analyst Cannot Do in Evaluation

The social analyst is of course firmly committed to an action view by the nature of his approach and subject-matter. He certainly cannot override or ignore the ideas of those with whom he works on what is valuable, or in what specific direction to pursue change. It is not up to him to judge after the event whether the situation is in fact better or worse as a result of change. And it is not up to him to decide whether or not new and unexpected things coming to light as a result of change actually constitute 'problems'.

Moreover, it is not up to the social analyst to insist that a systematic or comprehensive review is made of the consequences of deliberate change. If the actors with whom he is working themselves wish for systematic review (as happened in the particular hospital case-study described in Chapter 2) then there is no difficulty. The social analyst cannot, however, institute a systematic review on his own without undermining all belief in his affirmation of a collaborative-exploratory role, in contrast to that of 'objective' observer. It is not for the social analyst at any time to turn on the people with whom he has been working, as it were. It is not for him to make his own independent checks, measurements or observations of just what they have been doing; or what (in his own judgement) has resulted of significance.

In fact, to judge from experience, it is relatively unusual for organizational actors to desire systematic reviews of changes that have followed from social-analytic work. Why is this? It seems probable that it is because of the specific nature of the material under change – social institutions. For one thing there is the extreme diffi- culty (as discussed in Chapters 4 and 5), of even establishing clear facts about what the prevailing institutions 'are' at any given time. Exploration is likely to show familiar divergences between 'mani- fest', 'assumed' and 'requisite' views. And in addition to this (again, as discussed in Chapter 4), there is difficulty in principle in collecting factual data which have real relevance for judging the effects or effectiveness of social institutions. Thinking back to the hospital case- study quoted in Chapter 2, for example, can it be imagined that a count (were it possible) of the times when any of the three chief officers of the Hospital Group had a violent disagreement with each other, would give a useful indication of the adequacy of the defini- tion of their roles? Does either the incidence of staff turnover or the discharge rate of patients provide a useful measure of the adequacy of the defined roles and relationships of hospital doctors, nurses and other staff? Do the delivery times for orders, or the incidence of customer complaints, or even the level of recorded profits, give any reliable indication of the adequacy of the social structure of a fac- tory? In each case, the quality of the social institutions concerned may no doubt have an effect on these things. (Indeed, there would be little point in striving for better social institutions if they did not.) However, the linkages are so tenuous, the 'intervening variables' so profuse, that nobody but the most narrowly blinkered academic will consider that the systematic collection of such data for purposes of evaluation has any real value.

Certainly the actors concerned are unlikely to. The author can look back to an early experience in social-analytic work where he positively encouraged those embarking on organizational change – it happened to be in the nursing field – to carry out some degree of 'objective' evaluation. A series of systematic review-interviews were arranged to take place after six months' experience of a new organ- ization. An accompanying questionnaire was designed to get (amongst other things) a series of graded answers to the questions 'are you aware that any change has taken place?' and 'if so, has it been beneficial?' In the event there was a striking lack of interest in the accumulated 'data' from the coded answers to the questionnaire. The actors concerned obviously preferred to rely entirely on direct impressions gathered in the process of everyday work under the new structure, together with interchanges of views with each other in face-to-face discussion. The main concern in any case, it seemed, was not with how much things had changed, or with to what degree they had improved. It centred single-mindedly on this issue: is the present organization effective as it stands, and if not, what problems is it giving rise to?

The observable effects of social institutions are indirect. That is their very nature. Social institutions are frameworks for human decision and human action, and human action is always unpredictable. The question is not whether particular institutional forms *cause* particular observable consequences in practice, but whether experience proves them to be *consistent in principle* with various requirements which are held to be of prior importance. (This goes back of course to the basic idea of the 'requisite model' discussed in the previous chapter.) Thus harking back again to the case-study in Chapter 2, we cannot usefully inquire: does the right of the Secretary to the Hospital Management Committee to edit and submit all papers for the Committee inevitably cause him to come into conflict with the Treasurer? What we can inquire is whether this right is consistent with another 'given', which is the notion of the Treasurer as direct financial advisor to the Committee. Or, to take another example cited in the previous chapter, an organizational arrangement which involves physical separation might make it extremely difficult to provide an effective social work service to a hospital from a geographically distant Area Social Services office. However, who is to say if the staff are determined enough, and inventive in getting rapid communication and transportation that they might not after all make things work satisfactorily even in this difficult situation? All one can say in these or similar circumstances is that physical separation is, generally speaking, inconsistent with the development of close and continuous working relationships.

## The True Role of the Social Analyst in Evaluation

This point about consistency gives the clue as to the true role of the social analyst in evaluation, and as to what he may usefully do in practice. When people introduce new social institutions into their lives it appears to be the case that they do not in fact usually consider undertaking some systematic, factually based review or evaluation at some later date – not, that is, unless their soundly based instinct is disturbed by half-realized ideas about what constitutes a proper 'scientific' approach to change. (The positivist-minded researcher who is still unbelieving at this point may care to reflect on his own behaviour, and the assumptions implicit in it, the last time that he reorganized his own research unit!) What they tend to do in fact is simply to go on employing these institutions, that is acting within them, until such time as experience makes them aware of contradictions, whether they be contradictions with the requirements originally held, or contradictions with new requirements which have arisen. If they have been engaged in social analysis, it is at these points that they will often return spontaneously to the social analyst, and invite him to resume discussions. Then and only then, can the latter resume exploration on a collaborative basis. And then what he will in fact find himself doing is helping the actors concerned to review the consequences of previous changes, to identify new problems which have come to light, to tease out possibilities for further or extended action, and to reconsider or extend the relevant criteria against which these may be judged. In a broad sense of the term the social analyst will now indeed be heavily involved in 'evaluation', but the actual nature of his contribution will be no different in fact from what it was at the 'planning' stage. The view will have shifted from before-the-event to after-the-event, but his particular role will remain unchanged.

Thus change in social institutions following social analysis may certainly give rise to what may quite accurately be described as 'test' situations, but not to what might in any strict sense be described as 'experiments' or 'controlled experiments'. Apart from the lack already remarked on, of the possibility of providing experimental evidence in the form of hard data, the social analyst has simply no ability or right to insist that his collaborators hold steady their social institutions or any other conditions over some given period, perhaps in the face of mounting difficulties, all in the name of science. Nor has he the ability or right to instruct a number of others in similar or parallel institutional settings to do the same in order to provide comparative control-groups. (Indeed how far any of these things are ever realistic possibilities in institutional change, even outside a specific social-analytic approach, must be a matter of great doubt.)

As far as written accounts of this after-the-event phase of social-analytic work are concerned, there will be no detailed surveys of the factual effects of change, or of attitudes to it, to report; no tables of changes in 'disputes recorded', 'clients cared for', 'staff absences', 'income or profits earned', and the like. The hard core of any formal accounts of evaluation will be reports of where social institutions did *not* work; and following this, statements of why in the light of further exploration this appeared to be so, and what was then done to rectify the matter. Invariably, in fact, such accounts will not be published separately, but will stay embedded in more embracing descriptions of the particular projects concerned.

Take again, for example, the hospital case-study described in Chapter 2. This started from problems expressed by the three chief officers about the fundamental nature of their mutual working relationships. The result of the first phase of work was to clarify the various kinds of 'co-ordinative' and 'monitoring' relationships which were felt to be appropriate, and at a certain point a formal enactment of these was made in order to test them out in practice. However, although a review undertaken six months later confirmed that the steps that had been taken were in the right direction, it revealed much more concern with certain new problems that had now come to light. These included uncertainty about the ability of the Treasurer to make direct submission of financial reports to the Management Committee, and the problem of his apparently over-prescriptive relationship to junior nursing staff. And with these new problems, new objectives and criteria came into view. In addition to the desirability of creating good general working relationships between the three chief officers, there emerged, for example, the more specific requirement to maintain adequate financial control without undermining the direct accountability of the heads of various services.

Another example of this evaluative aspect of the social-analytic process can be taken from the Glacier Project. A published account[2] describes the various attempts to get a requisite formulation for the role of specialists in the company over the period from 1952 to about 1960. Between Divisional Managers in charge of major production divisions on the one hand, and the Departmental Superintendents under them in charge of specific production departments on the other, there was a whole array of such specialists: personnel managers, production controllers, chief production engineers, chief accountants, and so on. In the early days, the apparent situation was that these specialists had no authority in dealing with department production staff other than that of offering advice or providing services. In reality however, many of the pronouncements issuing from them on such things as manufacturing methods, prices and delivery schedules, were felt to carry a stronger force that that of 'advice'. The first attempt to clarify this situation with the help of social analysis centred round the specific concept of a 'prescription'. This was defined as the experts' way of tackling a problem or overcoming a difficulty. It was not a direct order to an operational manager, but simply offered to him at the initiative of the specialist concerned, or at his own request. 'Like a doctor's prescription, it could be refused by the patient, but of course at his own peril.'[3]

[2] See *Exploration in Management*, Part IV.        [3] *Exploration in Management*, p. 157.

With the official introduction of this new conception, specialists now found themselves with the task of persuading operational managers to accept 'prescriptions'. This still, however, felt greatly at odds with what the reality of the situation actually demanded. A further attempt was made to analyse and clarify the matter. It was gradually realized that one of the obstacles to progress had been the inability to distinguish the activity of giving instructions from that of being a manager. Explicit formulations were made of the idea of 'staff authority', this being the right to give instructions within the general brief or policy set by the overall manager. Staff authority was clearly differentiated from managerial authority, the latter including powers to assess personal performance, assign appropriate work in line with assessed capabilities, affect pay, and so on (none of which was relevant to staff authority). 'Specialist' groups were explicitly differentiated from 'operational' units, and members of the former were assigned clear 'staff officer' status.

By and large, these later formulations proved much more satisfactory in practice. However, one new major problem at least was thrown up by this second wave of changes, bringing the need for yet a further piece of analysis and clarification. One specialist group – the Commercial Division – as it was constituted, included a mixture of activities including production planning, pricing and accounting. Experience of the attempts to deal with all this as 'staff work' and to assign staff officer roles to all those who carried it out proved to offer difficulties. Further analysis showed that the activities of the Division were essentially of two kinds. One kind, 'programming activities', fitted well into the main specialist framework, finding its place alongside and complementing two other major specialist dimensions – 'technical' and 'personnel'. Experience showed however, that the second kind of work, accounting and financial work, did not fit well into this framework. Accountants did not happily act as staff officers. Their work, it seemed, was better conceived as part of a second system independent of the main operational or executive system, and primarily concerned with providing the Board of Directors and the shareholders with an independent account of the financial state of the company.

Thus over a period of seven or eight years or so, a gradual evolution of practice and understanding in this particular area of social institutions took place in the company concerned. At each stage explicit statements of the change involved, and of the new system which was to prevail, were made. However, the main point in this context was that at no stage was it felt relevant to make any systematic collection of factual data, or to undertake systematic 'attitude surveys' in order to evaluate the changes introduced. Where the shoe fitted there were no complaints and nothing further needed to be done. And where it did not fit, those affected were quick enough to voice the fact, without calling for 'objective' studies to help them make up their minds. What they were really looking for was not some objective measure of the adequacy of past changes, but further help in analysing new problems and developing possible lines of remedial action.

## The Place of Systematic Data Collection in Evaluation of Other Kinds of Change

The conclusion that systematic data collection has little place in evaluation of institutional change, joins up of course with the similar conclusion reached in Chapter 4. There we saw that systematic factual surveys offered little help either in the initial exploration of problems concerning social institutions, or in developing possible models for future change in them. As in Chapter 4 however, we must guard against jumping to the conclusion that systematic data collection has no contribution to make in any kind of collaborative exploration, or the evaluation of change which may result from it. On the contrary, we have only to consider two other fields identified in Chapter 4 in which deliberate change is possible – the field of technical change and the field of 'programming' – to discover scope for factual surveys in either planning or evaluation.

In the field of programming for example – the field of schedules, targets, budgets, cost-benefit analysis and so on – it is hardly possible to imagine adequate evaluation of change which could do without the systematic collection of hard data of some kind or other. Measures of such things as production levels, sales, orders received, clients dealt with, patients treated, children born, deaths, complaints, and so on, and so forth, as well as a variety of measures of costs and expenses, have to be gathered if informed judgements of past actions are to be made. In technical matters too, there is often scope for the collection of quantitative data to inform judgements of effectiveness – how successful a certain method is of teaching children to read, or treating some disease, or manufacturing a certain chemical. (In all these fields there are, of course, difficulties in principle in establishing exact measures of output or success wherever 'action' assumptions prevail, as for example in psychotherapy or higher education; but this is not to say that no factual data of any kind can ever be gathered which can genuinely help to inform judgements about achievement.)

It is not then that systematic data collection for the purposes of evaluation is always inappropriate in principle in real-life change situations. It is, to repeat the point, simply the nature of social institutions that makes the systematic collection of straightforward factual data largely irrelevant in assessing the effects or adequacy of change in them.

## The Validation of General Propositions

Let us turn now to the second question to be considered in this chapter, namely how the ideas arising from social analysis can be proved to have general validity. The question may be restated as follows: even if social analysis has led to changes judged to be beneficial in one particular setting, how can one be sure that the ideas on which these local changes are based have general application elsewhere?

Now it has already been established in Chapter 5 that what is involved at the heart of each specific piece of social-analytic work is some general formulation or proposition about social institutions, not merely a specific recommendation. Each and every project provides therefore an opportunity not merely to evaluate the applicability of particular solutions in particular cases, but to test the validity of these general propositions. Although it is not the business of the social analyst to evaluate particular actions, it is certainly his concern to validate general models and the conceptions on which they rest. Here the careful distinction between the words 'validating' and 'evaluating' is deliberate. 'Evaluating' means in the ultimate, attaching value to something. Validation, if it is to be a scientific process, must be value-free. It must that is, be a process in which the predictions of theory are tested against the facts of experience to see whether they pass or fail.

In other words, because and only because the method of social analysis involves the teasing out of general statements about social institutions and their relation to other factors of a general nature (in contrast to the specification of specific solutions to specific problems), every individual project, where enacted change occurs, provides in effect a scientific experiment. In each project the evaluation of specific actions for their practical use in the specific circumstances, and the testing of requisite propositions for their general validity, proceed hand in hand and simultaneously. The test for both is similar and essentially one of falsification: does experience reveal any specific (or general) inadequacy in the formulation, in the light of the specific (or general) requirements posited?

The more the situations in which general propositions are tested by deliberate, enacted change in this way, the more confidence can be held in their use and validity. (Although, as in all scientific endeavour, it is perhaps more useful to think of theories having not so far been proved wrong rather than having been proved right.) Moreover, continued work in one project area over perhaps a number of years, with several returns to more sophisticated analysis and refined solutions, provides a powerful opportunity not just to falsify, but to improve and refine, scientific theories.

However, although enacted change is the only ultimate test of social institutions, propositions about them may often be pre-tested as well to a considerable extent in general discussions. As we have said, requisite models of social institutions are not merely generalizations of empirical facts. They are also, to a significant degree, arguments about the internal logic of given sets of social requirements. Although in the end they can only be tested by direct enactment and use, they often describe situations which are already within the common experience of many social actors. Thus with suitably chosen people it is perfectly possible to undertake in general discussion a searching, critical analysis of the internal consistencies and fundamental implications of various alternative models, like those for medical practice for example, or for the provision of social work in hospitals, described in the previous chapter. Often in this way, much important, though preliminary, validation is carried out in social analysis. This indeed is a major function of the 'research conference' as a particular tool of social analysis, described in Chapter 7.

### The Evaluation of the Social-Analytic Endeavour Itself, and the Possible Place for a Third Party

We have been primarily concerned in this chapter with the role of social analysts in helping those with whom they work to evaluate changes that have been made as a result of social-analytic projects. We have not been concerned with the rather different matter of the evaluation of the work of social analysts themselves by those who employ or sponsor them. Nevertheless, the exploration we have just conducted in this former topic has some implications for the latter which are worth noting.

As was suggested earlier, those who are intent on evaluating the social-analytic endeavour itself will have to consider a number of separate elements. They will have to consider the extent and depth of the general scientific knowledge of social institutions which has accrued, and how far its validity has been proved. They will also have to consider how far this knowledge has influenced actual enacted change, and been judged beneficial in its effects. Overall, they will have to decide what weight they wish to give to scientific objectives in contrast to change objectives.

In considering all these things, sponsors obviously need direct access to the views of actors who have been involved in collaborative work (if they themselves are not the actors directly concerned). But for the reason described earlier, it will be as unrealistic in principle to expect to find useful 'hard' data to support this broader level of evaluation as it is for the evaluation of change in specific projects. This is not at all to imply that any evaluation of social-analytic work is either impossible or unwarranted. It is simply to note that all will rest ultimately on judgement, informed as it may be by close contact with written accounts of the work that has gone on, the scientific material that has accrued, and the personal responses of the various collaborating actors concerned.

Could some third party, some 'independent' evaluator, be of use here, either in evaluating local change or (thereby) helping to evaluate the social-analytic work itself? The answer here must be a firm negative. Again, the two potential components of any evaluative work must be considered separately: systematic data collection on the one hand, and analysis of outcomes, problems and the criteria for assessing them on the other. As far as systematic data collection is concerned, if there were any relevant data to be had, there would be no need to bring in a third party to collect it. The social analyst or those with whom he works could readily do so. However, as we have seen, there is usually no such relevant data where institutional change is concerned. As far as systematic analysis of outcomes, problems and criteria of judgement is concerned, this is precisely what, through collaboration, the social analyst is himself engaged in. If he does it badly, he should stop. Bringing in a third party could not possibly help, but only confuse. The social analyst is himself (or aspires to be) an 'independent evaluator' in this sense. Although he is prepared to become intimately involved in the problems of those with whom he works, he attempts at all costs to avoid becoming part of the system, and to retain a proper professional and scientific objectivity.

## Conclusion

To summarize then, evaluation is a normal part or element of the social-analytic process, but it has to be understood in a particular way. Given the subject field of the work (social institutions) and the particular method of work (collaborative exploration) which is most appropriate for getting to grips with it, neither systematic planned reviews of change, nor the large-scale systematic collection of quantitative or survey data, play any significant part in the process.

This is not a matter of whim or accident, but is absolutely consistent with the major premises. For the analyst to attempt to insist on a systematic planned review of outcomes following enacted change, other than any review spontaneously desired by those with whom he works, would be completely inconsistent with his avowed intention only to work where he is invited and in response to actual problems being experienced. And even when his help is specifically invited, for the analyst to insist on the systematic collection of hard data in order to judge the adequacy of institutional change would be quite inconsistent with the nature of enacted social institutions, which, as we have seen, simply do not permit this sort of aid to evaluation (unlike change in many other aspects of organized activity).

The role that the social analyst can play in evaluation of institutional change when he is invited to do so – and it is an important one – is threefold. First, he will help the actors concerned to explore and analyse the new problems they are experiencing following enacted change. Secondly, he will help them to reassess the validity of the criteria by which they were guided in the first place; that is, to reassess the values which they were bringing to bear. Thirdly, he will help them to expose the possibilities for ameliorative or further action.

As far as the choice of specific criteria or aims suited to the particular situation in question is concerned, the final decision rests, of course, with the immediate actors, not with the social analyst. This must be true both at the point of deciding future action, and at the point of assessing past ones. Nevertheless at some deeper level the social analyst cannot avoid intruding broader values of his own, whether consciously or not. In this particular sense then, but only in this sense, the social analyst too is an evaluator, a giver of value. It is to consideration of these broader values underlying the whole social-analytic approach that we now turn.

# 10 Underlying Values and Necessary Skills

It has constantly been stressed that it is not up to the social analyst to say what particular problems justify attention, what specific actions should be taken to remedy them, or whether any remedial actions taken have been successful in the event. This does not mean, however, that the social analyst can somehow manage to achieve complete neutrality on all matters of value, or indeed that he should even aim at this. Inevitably, in everything that he does, by subtle nuance or explicit statement, by what he omits to comment on as well as by what he says, he will be communicating something of his own feelings and attitudes. He himself is a social actor; and the idea that he should try to deny his own deeply held beliefs would be not only repugnant in itself but, in any case, in fundamental contradiction to the 'action' view of the world which he is upholding. The real point here is not to raise again the chimera of the value-free scientist, but to distinguish specific views about what other people should do in the specific situations in which they find themselves, from more general, underlying values to which the social analyst may wish to give expression. We come now to look more closely at these underlying values. This leads naturally to a related topic – the special skills and knowledge required of the social analyst.

## The Underlying Values and Beliefs in Social Analysis

The exact nature of the fundamental beliefs, values and convictions which the social analyst imports into discussion will obviously vary somewhat from individual to individual. Needless to say, there is no explicit code written or unwritten, to which everyone is under any obligation to adhere. Nevertheless, any prolonged exposure to social-analytic practice as it has grown, or any careful scrutiny of the published writing, cannot help but suggest that those who do the work share a certain broad outlook. (The word 'outlook' is used deliberately. At this depth any distinction between values and beliefs becomes pedantic: this is a level where the two merge.) It appears that something like six root beliefs or values exist, which may be summarized as follows.

### Idea of Man as a Free Actor

As has been stressed throughout the previous pages, one of the most fundamental assumptions in social analysis is that of man as a purposive, choosing, responsible actor. With this goes a belief in his right to make uncoerced choices (albeit within limits – *see* next item) and in this right as being an essential part of his human status and central to his satisfaction and personal growth. This is in sharp contrast to a 'behavioural' view, which sees man as an organism whose behaviour is simply to be conditioned or controlled by coercion, reward, physical manipulation, or the like.

As already noted, this view of man as a freely choosing actor, is broadly consonant with that of many of the so-called humanistic psychologists (Fromm, Maslow, Rogers and so on) and with the symbolic-interactionist and phenomenological schools of sociology (Mead, Schutz, Weber, etc.). It reflects something, though not all, of the outlook of the psychoanalytic tradition.[1] It shares something of existentialist philosophy and much of the outlook of the more libertarian political philosophers and commentators (J. S. Mill, the classical anarchist writers and latter-day figures like Popper, Berlin, Hayek and Dahrendorf). It is an approach therefore which claims a foothold in every department of social and political thought.

### Idea of Man as a Socially Controlled Being

Exactly complementing this first principle, and in no way in contradiction to it, is the idea of man as a social being, as a role-player. Man is seen as constantly assuming new positions in a multitude of differing social groups, each of these positions having specific rights and duties (more or less clear and agreed) attaching to it. These established roles limit, to a greater or lesser degree, the range of possible action freely available to him, but they do not remove or destroy it.

This view of man as a role-player is now a familiar one in social

---

[1] On what might be described as the uneasy mixture of 'action' and 'behavioural' assumptions in psychoanalysis, *see* Halmos (1965), *The Faith of the Counsellors*; Szasz (1974), *Ideology and Insanity*; and Rycroft (1968), *Psychoanalysis Observed*.

theory, although (as noted earlier) it is a view of comparatively recent origin. However, there is still a wide variety of ideas about exactly what is meant by the term 'role'. It is useful to distinguish what might be called the sociological concept of role as the rights and duties attaching to certain definite positions, from what might be called the social-psychological concept of role as observed regularity of social behaviour.[2] The latter is perhaps more consonant with a 'behavioural' than an 'action' approach. The sociological concept, which is the one we have taken, allows ample place for freedom of action. The particular expectations which make up the describable content of any role can be thought of as guides and limits to possible action, rather than as all-comprehending and freedom-denying prescriptions.

## Idea of Social Institutions as both Given and Changeable

This third idea follows immediately from the first two. Even though man is a social being conforming to given roles, being also a deliberative actor, he will tend to criticize these same roles, and seek to change them. The paradox referred to in Chapter 4 is in constant evidence. On the one hand social institutions have some factual reality at any time, which is open to systematic study. On the other they are always at the same time subject to the shifting, the blurring, between what is formally 'manifest', what is 'assumed' for the moment by each individual actor, and what each or all might wish to move towards as more 'requisite'.[3] Seen from another point of view, this amounts to an ever-present mixture of consensus and conflict. Without some consensus there would be no machinery at all for social dealings; without some conflict about this very machinery there would be no structural change.

In relation to the sociological controversy between 'consensus theorists' and 'conflict theorists',[4] social analysts have tended to be most frequently identified with the former camp by outside commentators. Thus, by implication or directly, they have been branded as essentially conservative and 'establishment-oriented' in outlook. (Other equally sweeping identification with the 'scientific management' school of thought, or sometimes with the psychoanalytic school, has sometimes been used to the same effect.)

[2] *See* Dahrendorf's review of this issue in 'Homo Sociologicus' (1968a).

[3] *See* again the important exposition of the dual, paradoxical nature of social institutions as both objective realities and subjective constructs in Berger and Luckman (1967), *The Social Construction of Reality.*

[4] Demerath and Peterson (1967), *System, Change and Conflict.*

Now it is true that social analysis directs its efforts to securing piecemeal, evolutionary change rather than wholesale revolution (*see* below). Nevertheless, to characterize it as concerned with simply maintaining or shoring-up the status quo is wrong. Not only change, but structural change, is a central concern in social analysis. Indeed, social analysis is positively radical in the way in which it introduces new definitions and interpretations, and thus new possibilities for action, into otherwise stagnating situations.

The social analyst expects to find conflict wherever he goes: it is his everyday bread and butter. He has no aspiration to remove all conflict or even to deny its efficacy. He is simply concerned to see if some degree of rationally based consensus on necessary institutions can be reached, within which further discussion, controversy and conflict may then flow more creatively. The social analyst can never afford to adopt a 'consensus' outlook to the exclusion of a 'conflict' outlook, or vice versa. He must employ both, simultaneously.

## Belief in the Evolution of Social Institutions by 'Piecemeal Social Engineering'

In quoting at the beginning of this book Karl Popper's famous phrase 'piecemeal social engineering' we are deliberately invoking many of the ideas that accompany it.[5] The first is the rejection of what Popper describes as 'Utopian engineering'. Like Popper, the social analyst assumes that it is both unnecessary and undesirable to think of foregoing all change until some Utopian order can be achieved in one great leap. Nor does he assume that making stern and sweeping denunciations of today's muddle achieves much in the way of practical results. The central metaphors are not those of ruthless demolition, radical planning and wholesale reconstruction. They are those of reclamation, cultivation and piecemeal development. Of course it has always to be recognized that there are some social situations in which men find themselves which are so repressive, pernicious and incapable of being changed by piecemeal development, that conflict or violence is the only recourse. Nevertheless, when the intolerable has been destroyed, the better society to replace it has still to be constructed by slow and patient effort.

[5] *See* Popper (1966), *The Open Society and Its Enemies*, and (1961), *The Poverty of Historicism*. (Quotations from the former work are reproduced at the beginning of this book.) There is an obvious and important link here too with the idea of 'disjointed incrementalism' in political change, expounded in Braybrooke and Lindblom (1963), *A Strategy of Decision*, and contrasted with what they describe as 'synoptic' or 'rational-deductive' approaches.

The instinct of the social analyst is to start with the here and now – to search for the seeds of the requisite amongst the chaff of the extant, so to speak. This does not mean that he never reaches out for broader speculations, or cannot by nature tolerate the thought of radical change. On the contrary, it is only by importing new speculations, new theories and new visions into everyday discussions that significant progress can be made. What it does mean is that in making his contributions to the exploration of any particular problem situation, he will remain conscious of what lies within the realm of possibility for those who are going to have to make changes in that situation (and to live with them thereafter).

A second idea implicit in 'piecemeal social engineering' is that of the deliberate introduction of new social institutions, their testing by failure or falsification, and their further modification in the lights of faults discovered. What is at issue is not simply piecemeal change; it is change which is *engineered*, in the sense that it is based on explicit scientific principles which can be tested, developed and extended as experience is gained. The term 'social engineering' catches something too of the constructive element in social analysis. Social analysis is concerned with making things work, or work better; in sharp contrast, for example, to the 'debunking' tone of much sociological theory.[6] Of course there is also a danger in the use of the term if 'engineering' is taken as implying (in line for example with the so-called 'scientific management' approach of the earlier decades of the century) a manipulative approach to social matters. It need hardly be stressed how foreign this would in fact be to the social-analytic ethos described here.

## Belief in Institutional Change Through Appeal to Reason and Equity

On the contrary the belief that change in social institutions should proceed by rational discussion amongst all the actors concerned, rather than by unilateral imposition of change by the most powerful, is another distinguishing mark of social analysis. Here again, there is

[6] 'We would contend then that there is a debunking motif inherent in sociological consciousness. The sociologist will be driven time and again by the very logic of his discipline to debunk the social systems he is studying,' '. . . . . every *Weltanschauung* is a conspiracy' (Berger, 1966, *Invitation to Sociology*, pp. 51, 78). 'Sociology operates . . . . . by questioning assumptions which seem to be made by people, and especially by people in authority in education, politics and so forth, about the behaviour of people . . . . . the practice of sociology is criticism' (Burns, 1970, 'Sociological Explanation', pp. 59, 72).

a sharp contrast to the general tenor of much sociological theorizing. The emphasis in social analysis is not on simply *interpreting* change in terms of the interplay of power and self-interest, but of *justifying* possible change in terms of appeals to agreed canons and criteria.

Analysis in terms of power or self-interest (as frequently employed in sociological discussion) may satisfactorily explain what is, but will never help elucidate what ought to be. Thus to take an illustration, analysis of inequality in society in terms of historical conquest, struggle for political control, possession of land or capital, and so forth, is one thing; analysis in terms of the existence of innate distinctions in human ability, or intrinsic differences in level in social functions to be carried out is another.[7] In principle analysis of this latter kind might (by most people's standards) form some possible basis for the justification of some degree of continued stratification. Analysis in terms of the former kind must logically leave any question of justification open. It is interesting to note that political theory and jurisprudence, in contrast to sociology, has always been more concerned with justifications, that is, with requisite forms of human institutions than with apparently 'neutral', causal explanations.

In social analysis, where the justification of particular forms of social institutions is always at issue, the criteria against which judgements are made are not, of course, simply those of the social analyst. Provided none of the basic values subscribed to by the analyst as described here are under attack, he will not be disappointed or think it irrational if one set of criteria rather than another is chosen by the actors with whom he is working. What is likely to disappoint him however, is the abandonment, for any variety of causes, of reasoned analysis of institutional needs and the introduction of arbitrary change with or without the ready agreement of all concerned.

## Belief in Social Problems as the Most Potent Source of Social Knowledge

Finally, we come to the belief which guides the social analyst's whole conception of the circumstances in which his work is most usefully commenced. This is the belief in starting where the most pressing problems are. Some of the advantages of a problem-oriented approach have already been described. First it makes for ready access

[7] *See* Bendix and Lipset (1967), *Class, Status and Power*, and Dahrendorf (1968d), 'On the Origin of Inequality among Men'.

for the searcher after social knowledge. Then it makes for commitment on the part of the actors involved to search diligently for the truth of the situation. They are, in the vernacular, 'playing for real'. Again, it allows the strongest possible test of the validity of the knowledge obtained; that is, the trial in practice of such knowledge by those who are anxious to make use of it. In summary, there is every reason to think that better, more valid, social theory results by starting from practical problems as defined by the actor-subjects, than by starting from theoretical issues as defined by the researcher.

However, there is an even deeper statement of the value here. By giving due attention to the needs or problems of those he is studying, the researcher is enabled to protect and indeed enhance his own humanity. He refuses to perceive any he works with as an 'it' to be 'objectively' studied, or even possibly manipulated, for the purposes of knowledge. He insists on seeing everyone of those with whom he works as a living 'thou' to be collaborated with, that is, to be in full communication with.[8] He refuses to be cast in the role of the pure, uncaring scientist. But he also refuses to be cast in the role of the pure unthinking helper. In adopting a scientific approach whilst responding to practical needs, he allows himself the possibility of remaining at the same time thinker and helper, scientist and activist.

## The Skills and Knowledge Required for Social Analysis

Here then are some of the assumptions and values underlying social-analytic practice. As has been observed, the actual weight given to any one of these will vary from person to person, but if by and large they do not seem sympathetic to the would-be practitioner, then he is probably best advised to try some other kind of work.

It is fitting at this point to make some brief observation about other characteristics that appear to be demanded of any would-be social analyst. By way of preparing the ground, it is perhaps useful to start in fact by noting some of the things which experience suggests are *not* of prime importance for the work. For example, although the social analyst is in a very real sense in the business of social research, it may be noted that skill in most of the conventional social research techniques – survey design, questionnaire design, statistical analysis and the like – is not, for the various reasons already fully gone into, of great relevance. Secondly, although some prior knowledge of the special characteristics of the particular field to which social analysis

[8] The contrast of the 'I–It' and the 'I–Thou' relationships in human affairs is drawn from Martin Buber's great study of this theme (Buber, 1970, *I and Thou*).

is being applied at any time is useful, it is not essential. It is not essential, for example, in order to do social-analytic work in industry to have actually worked in industrial production; or in order to do work in hospitals to be a qualified doctor or nurse. True, the analyst has to acquire a great deal of special knowledge about the particular field in which he is working at any time if he is to produce relevant analysis, even of a general kind. However, it has not usually proved beyond the ability of the otherwise capable analyst to pick up this knowledge in the course of his work.

What do appear to be the two basic and complementary skills necessary for effective work are in fact implicit in the definition itself of social analysis. The first is a particular kind of skill in dealing with people – the skill of the professional 'interventionist' or 'change agent'. It involves an ability to strike up easy relationships with a wide variety of people, and to be able to respond with sympathy and insight to their varying views of the world. This is a skill often to be found, for example, in those who have trained and worked as educators or social workers, counsellors or management consultants. The second is some deep understanding of the nature of social institutions: that is, it is a scientific ability. Here, one might expect to find ready recruits from those who had successfully undertaken formal studies in the social sciences, more particularly in sociology, anthropology or political studies; or even better, those who had also carried out research in these fields.

Experience has shown however, the considerable difficulty in finding recruits to social analysis who combine both these characteristics in strong measure. There appears in practice to be some natural polarization. Either the instinct to intervention, action and change is strong, and the ability to undertake genuine scientific conceptualization relatively weak; or the opposite holds. Of the two, some ability to form adequate relationships is essential for collaborative exploration. Without this, no productive work whatsoever can take place. Where this is present, but understanding and knowledge of the nature of social institutions are weak or lacking, the gap can be filled to some extent by induction to the specific ideas, concepts and models that have already accumulated from the project work at Glacier and Brunel (a process which takes something of the order of a year to complete). Unless however the analyst acquires somewhere along the way a deeper and broader appreciation of relevant social science and social philosophy, his mind is likely to be ill-prepared for the seeding and growth of genuinely new insights in the course of actual project work.

Intertwined with the existence of these two specific abilities or aptitudes is of course the question of the level of general matured ability of the analyst – in the terms of Elliott Jaques, of his actual 'capacity' at any stage of his career. Difficult though it may be to define this concept precisely, there is no doubt of its importance in considerations of the effectiveness of particular social analysts (as in many other questions). One aspect here is the capacity level of the analyst relative to those he works with. For example, however scientifically able he may be, and however open in his dealings with people of all kinds, it may be predicted that the social analyst in his early twenties is going to find some difficulties in establishing an effective analytic relationship with the fifty-year old managing director, director of social services, chairman of medical consultants, or national trade union official.[9]

Unlike the social worker, the teacher or the psychotherapist, the social analyst not only works for the most part with those of normal maturity, but, in many cases, with those of above normal ability or capacity. Moreover, as has been noted before, although social analysis can be and has been undertaken with those at all levels within organizations, there is a tendency for those at higher levels to become most deeply involved, given that they are the ones who usually carry the prime responsibility for devising organization. The shop-floor worker or learner-nurse may be interested in the way social institutions are shaped: the senior industrial manager or chief nursing officer has to be, if he is worth his salt. Obviously, the level of ability or capacity demanded here is not simply a function of age. Nevertheless, it may be suggested that those who undertake social analysis are unlikely to achieve full professional maturity in this work until perhaps their middle thirties or early forties.[10]

[9] Some of the other general factors beside individual capacity which bear on the ability of change-agents to create and maintain effective relationships with their clientele are analysed in Dale (1975), *What Is Organization Development?*, Chapter 7.

[10] For a more detailed description of the theories on the basis of which the ideas in these last two paragraphs are developed, *see* Jaques' hypothesis of the existence of discrete strata of capacity in the human population (Jaques, 1965a), and the extension by Rowbottom and Billis of this idea in their detailed description of five corresponding strata in all organized work (Rowbottom and Billis, 1977). Is there a lowest stratum at which would-be social analysis could be expected to work with full adequacy and scientific creativity? Is there a minimum separation of the capacity-stratum of analyst and co-actor if collaborative exploration is to become a reality?

# 11   Social Analysis in Overview

We have seen that social analysis is an activity characterized by three interlocking concerns: a concern with social institutions, a concern with scientific understanding of them, and a concern with developing the sort of understanding that has application to immediate practical problems.

We have seen that the institutions susceptible to this kind of approach are pre-eminently those to be found in organizations or organized groups of various kinds. In fact organized activity, including law-making, is the very area where it is possible for men to plan deliberately, indeed scientifically, the social institutions they need to achieve their many purposes. The forms of organized activity may be exceedingly diverse – from the largest state or private corporation to the family business or the partnership; from the commercial company to the professional association, trade union or club. However the actual elements of institutional life which may in principle be made the subject of enacted change are strictly limited in number. Enacted change may be made in the *structure* and *composition* of organized groups, in the *authority* or *accountability* or *perquisites* attaching to various positions, in the *functions* to be undertaken in various groups or in individual positions, and in various *rules* or *procedures* to be followed.

There are of course many other aspects of the life of organized bodies and groups in which change may occur: in prevailing values or ideologies, in personal attitudes, motivations and abilities and so on. Important though these things undoubtedly are, and desirable though changes in them may be, the point has been made that such things are not susceptible to change by deliberate enactment. (However it has also been noted that there are two other aspects of organized activity in which, as in social institutions, change may be made by deliberate choice and explicit decision: the first is the methods or technologies to be employed, and the second is the general area of 'programming' – *see* Chapter 3.)

We have seen also that in a scientific approach to social institutions the pre-eminent mode of work is not likely to be that of the systematic collection of factual data, generalized into the causal 'law'. The very nature of social institutions is such that the availability of 'facts' about them, other than those of the most straightforward kind, is likely to be severely limited. Moreover, the very idea of scientifically predictable, predetermined activity, is fundamentally at odds with that of social institutions. Social institutions are not precise machines in which human behaviour is inexorably processed. They are frameworks – rough and ready, and in process of constant alteration – within which freely chosen, and therefore to that extent unpredictable, human actions take place. Requisite models of social institutions are not statements which predict with certainty that particular purposes will be satisfied if particular forms are adopted. They are statements of particular forms which are *consistent* with the pursuit of these purposes.

We have seen how, given the particular nature of the subject matter in hand, an approach which may be characterized as 'collaborative exploration' rather than 'objective study' becomes the appropriate way of forwarding scientific understanding and at the same time, facilitating change. In this, the role of the social analyst is an elucidatory one. He is exclusively concerned, whether in the initial or in the so-called 'evaluation' phase, with eliciting information relating to experienced problems, with helping to analyse needs and aims, and with helping to expose and clarify possibilities for change. His job is not to offer or advise particular solutions, but rather to tease out formulations of various institutional models which would be requisite given certain constraints and needs. In the course of this, much attention will have to be devoted to clarifying the language in which such formulations are phrased, and the conceptions which they embody. Though the social analyst will necessarily bring certain underlying beliefs and values of his own to this process, it will not be part of his role to suggest or press particular objectives, or to argue the need for particular changes.

We turn now to the final issue to be considered – how far there is scope for a more extensive use of social analysis, as we have now described it, or of some of the ideas associated with it. Before considering this, it is appropriate to attempt at least some broad assessment of the general effect of social-analytic work undertaken in various settings up to the present time.

## Assessment of the General Effects of Social-Analytic Work So Far Carried Out

Surveying the extent of development so far, one is struck with simultaneous and conflicting impressions of success and failure. Considered all together, the work at Glacier Metal, in the National Health Service and in local authority Social Service Departments amounts to one of the largest, if not the largest, endeavours in organizational action research ever to have taken place. By itself the work at Glacier Metal presents a most remarkable achievement, stretching as it does over nearly thirty years of continuous analysis, change and re-analysis of virtually every aspect of the enacted social institutions of a large industrial undertaking. At the same time the sobering fact stands, that in no other industrial or commercial company has fully developed social-analytic work of any significant extent or duration been requested or supplied – and this in spite of the vigorous proselytizing work of the Glacier Institute of Management and the continuing series of publications expounding the project findings which has achieved world-wide distribution.

Then again in the health and social services work, there are many signs that the continuing stream of project work, conferences and publications for approaching a decade have begun to make a significant impact on national thinking. There is, for example, clear evidence of use of the outcome of the early social-analytic work in hospitals to be found in the detailed plans for the reorganization of the National Health Service which was introduced in 1974.[1] There is evidence (if less readily demonstrable) of the influence of social-analytic publications on the major reorganization of many Social Services Departments throughout the country, following wholesale change in the local authority system carried out in the same year.

Nevertheless, amongst all the many and various field projects undertaken in health and social services, there is no one project which can be pointed to where a sustained and repeated cycle of analysis, enacted change and subsequent re-analysis, has become an established feature, as was the case with Glacier Metal. There is (at the time of writing) no one site where the sort of continuity of work and comprehensive linkage with a whole social entity, which is

[1] Many of the basic conceptions and formulations used in the official publication *Management Arrangements for the Reorganized National Health Service* (Department of Health and Social Security, 1972) show clear links with those expounded in *Hospital Organization*. Members of the Health Services Organization Research Unit had regular contact with the Working Party which produced the former document.

advocated in Chapter 7, has really been achieved. (It could perhaps be argued in the case of the health service work that the prime entity concerned was the National Health Service itself; that on this view, continuity and comprehensive linkage had to a large degree been successfully achieved; and that a considerable degree of testing and reformulation had been achieved as well, at least through the medium of the continuing research conference programmes if not elsewhere. But this would still not meet the point about the need in the end of actual enacted change and test in specific sites and settings, based on specific pieces of social analysis.)

Some guesses about the reasons for this situation can be hazarded. It appears that truly productive social-analytic work requires a very special combination of circumstances. For a start, it requires that a significant number of the dominant or leading figures in the social setting concerned are deeply committed, and remain so over a period of years, to a process of patient, thought-out and deliberate institutional change. The key people must be by nature of an analytic cast. Indeed beyond this it is likely that they, as collaborators in a science-based endeavour, must have more than an average share of sheer scientific curiosity in social matters as well. (Social analysis, we must remember, is not simply a problem-solving activity, but a form of scientific research.)

It demands moreover that these key figures find themselves with the power and the opportunity to proceed in this way. It presupposes that they are not for example subject to some higher authority which is simultaneously imposing changes according to its own and very different patterns of thinking, or one that simply blocks any significant attempts at local experimentation. For in effect what is required is the opportunity to develop gradually a whole new organizational culture (as happened at Glacier Metal): one in which an ethos of widespread participation exists; one in which due recognition is given by all the people involved to the value of building and maintaining good social institutions; one in which the importance of a truly scientific approach in social affairs is recognized and accepted.

Finally, effective social-analytic work demands that the analysts concerned are themselves highly capable at their work, of a level of capacity and maturity to match those they work with, and willing to commit considerable personal stakes to the work over many years.

Given the daunting combination of pre-conditions, it is perhaps not surprising that the paradigm of social-analytic work described in previous chapters is so rarely achieved in practice. However, this does not by any means imply that lesser attempts or achievements have been or are worthless. For one thing, it obviously can never be known in advance just how ripe the conditions are for achieving or approaching the ideal mode of work in any particular circumstances which present themselves. Without the opportunity for frequent trials in varied settings the odds on success would be dangerously narrowed. For another, there is no doubt that more restricted work, particularly if it is reinforced by other parallel explorations and by research conferences, can still make a valuable contribution. Preliminary formulations can be developed, compared with those in similar settings, tested and modified in conferences. Ranges of emerging models of possible practice can be widely disseminated (with due caution as to their ultimate validity) and thus help to nourish and influence general thinking throughout the field concerned about possibilities for future changes on either a grand or a domestic scale.

## Scope for Further Developments

What then is the scope for a more extensive use of social analysis, or for some of the ideas associated with it?

If we start with the second part of the question, the vistas seem broad indeed. There appears to be great potential use for many of the actual findings which have already resulted from social-analytic work. Whatever the arguments about the fundamental principles of the approach, it can hardly be denied that a very considerable range of precise, practical and, in many cases, tested models of organizational structure and practice have emerged from it. With suitable introduction, many of these are readily available for immediate application in a wide variety of organizational settings by those who already have direct responsibilities for institutional design and change – industrial managers, personnel specialists, senior public officials, organizers of trade unions, voluntary or charitable associations, and so on. Indeed, following the publication of many books and articles, and the provision of a variety of courses and conferences, there are already some indications that a degree at least of widespread diffusion of this kind is beginning to take place.

Management consultants and others like them who offer concentrated held with organizational problems on a fee-charging basis could also readily use many of these findings. Given the nature of their practice, there is probably little opportunity for making significant advances in scientific discovery, conceptualization and test.

However, there is every reason to use whatever valid scientific knowledge is generally available.

Beyond this, there is considerable scope for more widespread use of some of the basic principles and practices in the social-analytic approach itself. Any of those, for example, whose work involves attempts to gain systematic and reliable knowledge of human attitudes, views, or assumptions, which lie below the surface of directly observable fact, might usefully ponder on the practice of feeding back written statements of discussion or interviews to those who were the subject of them. In this way both the validity of the formulations and the acceptability of publication in the form in which they stand can be tested simultaneously. Apart from this, it is likely that the work of all who practise as independent change-agents – not just analysts of social institutions, but management consultants, operational researchers, technical consultants and the like – could benefit enormously by explicit adoption of the 'collaborative exploration' approach described in Chapter 4, in contrast to the reliance on the traditional trilogy of 'fact-finding', 'diagnosis' and 'recommendation'.

Finally then, we come to the question of a more extensive practice of social analysis itself. Here it must be stressed again that there is more at issue than the offer of consultancy or help by an independent change-agent. One is speaking of an activity which is scientific in the sense of seeking to create genuinely new scientific insights and theories, and not just in the sense of applying existing ones. Such work is indeed research, whatever its accompanying practical benefits. It needs financing for periods of many years at a time. It also requires the stimulation of an intellectual climate likely to be found only in a university or similar academic institution.

Clearly, the scope for extension here is much smaller than that for a more widespread use of the products of social analysis as such, or for a greater adoption of some of the principles of its approach. Nevertheless, the widespread dissemination and use of social-analytic findings is only going to flourish in the long run if it is constantly nourished by some continuing sources of new ideas. This means there must be a certain number of academic centres where full-scale social-analytic work is and continues to be undertaken. There is certainly no shortage of room for further expansion. Even given the wide range of organizational fields already covered by social-analytic study, there are still plenty more yet untouched. Nor is there any reason why social analysis should not be tried out in many more centres of social research than those very few in which it is currently undertaken. The main thing is the emergence of suitable and interested would-be practitioners, given that they are prepared to recognize the need for some preparatory training, and the extent and length of the commitments they need to make to those with whom they offer to work.

For any already engaged in social science who might consider trying some social-analytic work themselves, a number of powerful attractions can be cited, as we have seen. One is the importance of the field of work – organized social institutions in modern society – a field, moreover, in a state of comparative underdevelopment at the present time. Another is the ready access to problems of rich interest, and the opportunity to experience a process in which theory, empirical research and actual change are firmly united. A third is a mode of research which views fellow men not just as passive entities to be studied and manipulated, but as social co-actors whose confidences are to be respected, and whose own ideas and choices are to be given full weight.

Can social science afford to ignore a method which offers such prospects?

# Appendix A. Specimen Project Reports

As discussed in the previous text there is little use of systematic surveys or the wide-scale collection of quantitative data in social analysis (*see* Chapters 4 and 9). The basic research record is the *project report* – a document based on discussions with either an individual or a small group in connection with some problem concerning social institutions, which has been posed by the group. Any report may contain a mixture of four main elements:

(1) Statements of the starting issue, and any further elaborations of problems experienced.
(2) Statements of certain clear-cut factual material which help to fix the starting situation (including perhaps quotations of *manifest* statements of the organization or institutions which prevail).
(3) Exploration and analysis of various working assumptions about the institutions that actually prevail and about the functions to be pursued.
(4) Formulations of possible requisite institutional models, and their relationship to certain given needs and constraints.

When reports have been discussed and cleared with the individuals or groups concerned, material in them is available for quotation or use in some broader forum, and eventually (if agreed) for public release. Researchers may, in addition, keep their own personal notes of discussions or observations, but no material of this kind will be publishable until it too is 'cleared' with the actors concerned.

There is not, nor could there be, any standard format for reports. Particular examples of reports will necessarily reflect to a large degree the individual style and method of work of the analyst concerned. The ultimate goal is objective scientific knowledge, but the path to it offers a number of choices and demands much exercise of judgement.

## Specimen 1

The first specimen produced below is a typical report of an initial discussion with one individual in connection with what, as far as its terms of reference are concerned, seems a relatively clear-cut project (Para. 1).

The report is based on one two-hour discussion which took place in the hostel concerned. It involves a person who is not, by the nature of her work, used to complex or sophisticated discussion of organizational issues. Nor has this particular person been involved in previous social-analytic exploration. Consequently, the report is relatively short and straightforward – in keeping with the principle of 'staying at all times with the actors' (Chapter 5).

A couple of straightforward factual matters are mentioned (Paras. 2 and 7). Some problems are exposed (Paras. 4, 6 and 10). A degree of preliminary exploration and analysis is introduced (Paras. 3 and 10). A first attempt is made to explore a possible model of the Residential and Day Care Officer being in a full managerial role to heads of establishments, and some of the consequences of this (Paras. 5 and 6). (The existing concept of 'managerial role' had been introduced and explored for its relevance in the course of discussion.) Two possible alternative models of procedures for 'placing' would-be residents in care are briefly considered (Paras. 8 and 9).

### RESIDENTIAL AND DAY CARE PROJECT
*Report of Discussion with the Matron of a Hostel
for the Mentally Subnormal*

1. This is a note of a first discussion directed to the following terms of reference set by the Project Steering Committee within the Department:
   1.1 to develop a detailed role specification for Residential and Day Care Officers;
   1.2 to obtain specification of major decisions to be taken by staff in respect of clients and to establish the respective discretion of central office establishments or staff of Area Offices to make such decisions.
2. Your Hostel accommodates 15 mentally subnormal girls of age 16

and upwards. The care staff consists of yourself, an assistant matron and one other.

*Role of the Residential and Day Care Officer (R&DCO)*

3. The role of the R&DCO is gradually emerging, but at the moment is still largely concerned with problems of material provision – with provision of equipment and maintenance of buildings. You point out that it is impossible to make a valid separation between quality of care and quality of physical provision on the one hand, and staffing and staff relations on the other, because all three interlock so closely.

4. At the moment there are a number of workers in the Department who may comment in the course of their work on the quality of care provided for residents, for example any visiting social worker; but there is no one person who seems prepared to take full responsibility for the activities as a whole, of the Hostel.

5. It is possible to see an R&DCO playing a full managerial role, provided that the occupant of such a post were sufficiently well qualified or experienced in work with the mentally handicapped. Such a person would shoulder accountability for dealing with all unresolved problems, whether they concerned individual residents, the general standard of care, staffing, or physical provision. Conversely, such a manager would have authority to give instructions and to assess the quality of work carried out – much as does a matron in respect of the work of a nursing officer in a hospital setting.

6. It would be possible also for such a manager to play a much needed role in providing as it were 'outside' recognition of the work of the staff of the establishment on behalf of the Department as a whole. Many of the staff – cooks and domestic staff as well as care staff – play a responsible role year in year out, often undertaking activities over and above their strict terms of reference. Because of the present uncertain managerial links with the Department as a whole, such tends to pass without due recognition at the moment, either at an informal level or in terms of more formal assessment of possible potentiality for progress or promotion.

*Placement*

7. At the moment all placements are co-ordinated by a social worker in the Area Office who worked previously in mental health. Any vacancies arising are reported to her, and suggestions for new residents to fill them come back from her.

8. If placements were left for the social worker concerned to arrange by direct contact with the various heads of establishments 'easy' placements would readily be made, but there is no saying that lower-grade or difficult cases would be equitably distributed amongst establishments.

9. Another possibility would be for the R & DCO to co-ordinate all local

placements. If he were in a managerial role, placement work would provide a natural extension. Clients who could not be placed locally, he would have to refer to Central Office.

*Relation with Social Workers*

10. It is not clear whether in principle, social workers should completely hand over control of the case, together with full case records, on placement. Subnormality placements tend in any case to be long term. In the normal course of things, the residential head has to do much work with relatives and with doctors. Should emergency admission to hospital be required, action inevitably rests with the Matron. Without possession of the case records, referral to a psychiatrist, for example, can be difficult.

## Specimen 2

The second specimen reproduced below is a typical report of group discussions which followed individual discussion with each of the members. The project concerns mechanisms for the control of 'intake', that is for dealing with the bombardment of initial approaches and referrals, in a local authority department concerned with children's problems. (The project is the one briefly described as 'Situation 3' in Chapter 3.) The local authority agency concerned was at the time of the report on the verge of merging into a general purpose 'Social Services Department'.

The terms of reference and exploratory steps that have already been taken are mentioned in Para. 1, and there is little need to add further descriptive or factual material from the point of those concerned. They know the general problem and they know the surrounding circumstances. Reports from individuals have been cleared and are available for others to examine if they wish to do so. This report summarizes the main issues.

Detailed problems exposed in the course of exploration are mentioned in Paras. 4 and 15. Some brief conceptual clarification of 'intake work', 'intake control' and 'emergency work' is introduced in Para. 3. Using these concepts, the relation of 'duty' systems and 'intake' systems is analysed (Para. 4); the possibility of control of work through categorization or other means is analysed (Paras. 5 and 6); the idea of 'pure assessment' is analysed, its inadequacy shown (Para. 7), and a more adequate concept introduced (Para. 8). Three alternative organizational models for intake work in the Area Office Team to be established in the new Social Services

Department are put forward, and some of the general criteria against which they may be measured are brought out (Para. 9).

## REPORT ON INTAKE CONTROL

*Introduction*

1. Following a meeting between the Casework Supervisor of the Children's Department and the Brunel research team, it was agreed that the views and opinions of relevant individuals with regard to deciding control mechanisms for intake be explored. This report is based on interviews with the Casework Supervisor, the Senior Child Care Officer and six Child Care Officers from the Intake Team, and on a group discussion that followed the draft report.

2. The discussions with the interviewees revealed varying degrees of consensus and disagreement. This report will deal first with criteria within the context of which structural and organizational alternatives can be discussed, next with possible organizational structures and their implications, and finally with some miscellaneous problems raised.

*Basic Definitions*

3. The following definitions may be noted:
   3.1 by 'intake work' we mean the reception, assessment, referral for further action, or closure, of all new incoming cases;
   3.2 by 'intake control' we refer to mechanisms for controlling the rate of incoming cases, and consequently the total caseload of the department;
   3.3 by 'emergency work' we mean action to deal with all emergencies, at whatever time, on new or existing cases.

*Specialist Intake Work*

4. One fundamental problem raised during the discussions was that of specialist versus general assessment. Is there a need for a separate intake group, specializing in assessment, or can this work be absorbed into the duty system? If one opts for the latter, duty officers would handle both intake work and emergency work, and all new incoming cases would presumably go to seniors for allocation to the long-term groups. If one opts for the former, the relationship between a duty system and an intake group must be considered. The general assumption was that intake control is best handled by specialist intake workers.

5. The question under discussion was couched in very general terms 'control mechanisms for intake'. In fact, all the respondents chose to restrict their comments to the situation presently appertaining in the department. There were no suggestions that intake control is best achieved by judging all intake cases against a list of detailed

categories. Such categories could be useful and necessary for statistical purposes, but whether they could ever be wholly realistic if used for control purposes is another matter. It seems from the lack of any suggested categories that there are not felt to be any which would be sufficiently hard and fast as to enable their use in prescriptive control of intake.

6. Detailed control categories being considered unworkable, judgements on needs and priorities on particular cases necessarily have to be left to individual intake workers. This discretion was seen as being best limited by an adequate system of supervision; not that intake workers should be subjected to case by case scrutiny over their decision, but that they should have available someone to whom to turn for advice and consultation on different cases, to review their work if required, and to provide general consultation on assessment technique.

*Balancing Needs and Resources*

7. The distinction between 'client needs' and the 'Department's resources' figured frequently in the discussions. There was some notion of 'pure' assessment, i.e. one based solely on the client's needs, as opposed to being based on knowledge of what resources the Department could offer. If this distinction were realistic, and assessment was made independently of the state of resources, there would obviously be severe problems of control. The rate of incoming cases would bear no relation to the rate at which the Department could absorb such cases.

8. In reality, assessment of a case involves three stages:
   8.1 establishing need for help;
   8.2 deciding whether the need is of the sort for which the Department caters;
   8.3 deciding whether the Department's resources in their present state of availability are suitably employed on this case.

This third decision is crucial to assessment. Some knowledge about, for example the availability of caseworkers, or the availability of places in homes, is essential. Of course, this knowledge may vary in its accuracy, but to talk of 'pure' assessment, with no reference to resources, is to see assessment as being only the first and second stages, and to ignore the reality of actual intake practice.

*Suggested Criteria for Organization of Intake Work*

9. Several criteria for achieving control emerged from the discussions, and it will be with reference to these that possible structures will be examined. It was agreed that intake workers need:
   9.1 to have a constant flow of information about the current state of the Department's resources, including details of caseload size and vacancies in homes;
   9.2 to have as extensive a knowledge as possible of community and

local resources, particularly information about voluntary and other agencies that can provide alternative services to those offered by the Department;

9.3 to have available specialist consultation and discussion of cases and assessment technique;

9.4 to receive regular feedback from long-term groups concerning action taken on cases referred to them, to highlight any inconsistencies in the assessments of intake and long-term workers;

9.5 to receive detailed information about what has happened to those cases that intake has not accepted in the past.

*Alternative Structures*

10. The assumption has already been made that specialist intake workers are necessary for adequate intake control. On the further assumption that they would work within the context of Area Teams in the future combined Social Services Department, there is a problem of exactly where they should fit in. Assuming that the social workers in an Area Office are accountable to the Area Officer for their work, with the senior social workers (Team Leaders) exercising essentially supervisory and consultative functions, intake specialists could be incorporated in several alternative ways.

11. Although intake control has hitherto been taken to mean all intake, different Area Officers may wish to include all, or only part, of the incoming cases in their intake control procedures. Different kinds and different rates of incoming cases would be the deciding factor in the choice of which alternative the Area chose.

12. The first alternative that has been suggested is that intake social workers might work with whichever team leader (senior) was the 'duty' team leader. In terms of the criteria mentioned above, this suggestion would make it difficult to provide intake specialists with sufficient feedback on resources, and with opportunities for consultation or supervision. This model implies a division between intake on the one hand, and the 'duty' or emergency system on the other.

13. In the second, specialist intake social workers would have their own permanent intake team leader to provide them with consultation and supervision, and all feedback information could be channelled through one person only, the team leader. This model also provides for the possibility of the emergency duty system being in the hands of the intake team.

14. However, in view of the limited staff resources available to Area Officers in the new Social Services Department, this second model would be difficult. It is unlikely that an Area Officer could afford to have one out of his or her three or four team leaders employed fulltime on intake work. To overcome this one of the team leaders who already had a team of long-term caseworkers might take responsibility for intake work as well. This Team Leader could either have a

team composed of some intake workers and some long-term case-workers, or a team of intake specialists who also have some long-term caseloads.

## Miscellaneous Problems

15. Finally, several other problems associated with intake control emerged from the discussions:

   15.1 Should the doors of the Department be open to all, or should there be some prior control through, for example, previous approval by general medical practitioners, or through appointments systems?

   15.2 Given the need for some social workers to be designated intake specialists, what specific personal qualities do they need? What are the differences between intake and long-term caseworkers?

   15.3 Does one aim to keep the initial interview as short as possible in order to lessen client contact with a social worker who might not continue with the case? Or does one aim to devote as much time as possible to the client in the hope that sufficient ground will be covered to prevent the need for any further contact in many cases?

   15.4 Should intake specialists carry long-term cases and, if so, in what proportion?

   15.5 How adequate are the present recording mechanisms and do they facilitate control and review by the supervisor? Is the right information being recorded, and is it being used to the best advantage? Is enough known about those refused the Department's help, and what happens to them afterwards?

   15.6 How does one avoid giving undue attention to claimants who shout most loudly at the expense of the less forthcoming, whose real need may be greater?

## Specimen 3

The final specimen is a report of neither an initial discussion with an individual, nor a group discussion immediately following such individual discussions. It records two discussions undertaken at their specific request with a group of three senior staff members from a Social Services Department, one of whom is the Director.

The main issue under consideration is how best to incorporate and organize a number of hospital social workers in a large psychiatric hospital, a large general hospital and some smaller hospitals, who are due to be transferred as a group to the Department from the National Health Service. Detailed project work has already been undertaken with many of these social workers and some initial reports and ideas have been made available. All three of the senior staff taking part in these immediate discussions are familiar with this earlier work, and also with the general social-analytic approach, so that many corners can be cut. Also (in contrast, say, to the recipient of the first report) they are all well used to dealing with complex organizational issues.

Thus, a variety of different problems have been covered and analysed in discussion: the fundamental relation of social work to medicine (Para. 2); problems of record-sharing (Para. 6.1); how exactly to incorporate the newly acquired social workers into the Departmental organization (Para. 8); and even some problems of bringing about change (Paras. 4, 6 and 11).

Two kinds of defined conceptual models are used. Firstly, there is the idea of *managerial* and *co-ordinative* roles (Para. 7) with which these particular participants are already familiar. Secondly, there is a general theory or conception about stratification in work (also Para. 7) which has been developed elsewhere and which is being tried out in discussions in this particular setting for the first time. Alternative organizational models are introduced (Para. 8), and some brief analysis of their appropriateness in relation to basic criteria is undertaken (Paras. 9 and 10). (A more extended discussion of models of hospital social work and the criteria against which they may be ranged is to be found in Chapter 8.)

## ORGANIZATION OF HOSPITAL SOCIAL WORK

1. These notes record some of the main points touched upon in two discussions on 28th May and 10th June.
2. One fundamental consideration is whether hospital social workers (medical or psychiatric) are considered essentially as *aides* to doctors or as professionally *independent*. If the second view is favoured, there is an implication that their fieldwork will be distinct from that of doctors (including psychiatrists). It would presumably have more to do with mediating the patient-client's relationship to his normal physical and social environment (occupation, home, family, etc.) than with working directly on the patient's physical or mental condition. There is an implication that the social worker's role in the therapeutic team may be distinct and not normally interchangeable with that of other members (this has bearing, for example, on the question of social worker's taking on a primary therapist role, as described in the Psychiatric Hospital report).
3. The second view also implies that the hospital social worker would not be organizationally subordinate to the doctor. However, in health settings the doctor is still the primary professional, and the

social workers are the secondary professionals. This means that the doctor will have prime responsibility for cases and thus carry a co-ordinative role in relation to other professionals.

4. It is recognized that there may be problems in bringing hospital workers to a different view of their role in some cases as they are incorporated into the Department. Arranging for community social workers to work part-time in hospitals alongside existing hospital social workers was noted as one way, but by no means the only way, to this end.

5. As members of the Social Services Department, it was noted that hospital social workers are now eligible to assume certain responsibilities (e.g. for finding somewhere or other suitable accommodation for discharged patients who were lacking it; for taking action in battered baby cases), which formerly did not and could not rest with them.

6. In considering long-term possibilities for development and change in this field, it was noted that whilst hospital social workers are now under the ultimate control of the Department, doctors are not. Although it may be possible to influence medical practice to some degree, by and large social work in this sphere will inevitably have to be shaped to medical practice as it actually exists and independently develops.

    6.1 In thinking of questions of information-sharing and confidentiality, it is clear that *medical* records are under the control of doctors, but *social work* records (including those kept by hospital social workers) are now under the control of the Department.

    6.2 Since GPs are, and continue to be, important participants in every medical case even where medical specialists are heavily involved, it seems highly unlikely that *one* group of social workers who are hospital-based will ever be able to deal with all medical cases at all stages, pre- and post-hospital.

7. A three-level model of work was explored for its relevance to the

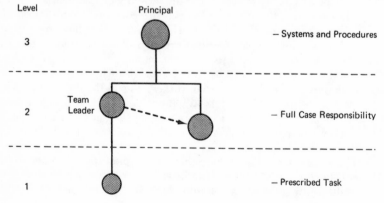

hospital social work situation. In Level 1 the tasks are prescribed. Trainees, students and case-aides may be at this level; also perhaps more junior or inexperienced basic-grade workers (though the latter will undoubtedly be rehearsing, if not carrying full responsibility for, work conceived in Level 2 terms). At Level 2, workers will carry full case responsibility with full authority to decide their own tasks. Senior graded hospital social workers will be at this level, and probably some of the more experienced basic-grade workers. The senior might *co-ordinate* but would not *manage* the work of other workers in their teams at this level. At the third level, staff would carry full managerial accountability for the work of Level 2 and Level 1 workers, and would be concerned with organizing and developing the total *system* of work. It is possible that the work of some or all existing hospital Principal Social Workers might lie at this level.

8. Three main possibilities for organization of on-site social work in hospitals have been identified:

8.1 Separate hospital team with own Level 3 manager

8.2 the outposting of Level 2 worker or workers to small hospitals from existing hospital teams of type 8.1, if they exist;

8.3 the outposting of Level 2 workers specializing in hospital social work from existing community social work teams, one of whom would take a co-ordinating role within the hospital.

9. Because of the need to have a relatively large staff on-site, dealing with urgent work as it arises, and providing an integrated cross-hospital group service, it seemed that the first model might be most appropriate for the General Hospital.

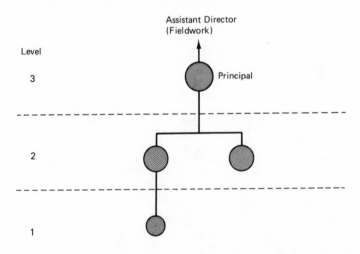

10. Because of the predominantly geographical organization of work and the increasing chances of hospital workers continuing to work with

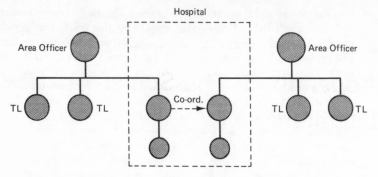

discharged patients or out-patients in the community, it seemed that
the third model might be best for the Psychiatric Hospital.

11. Finally, it was noted that what was the most desirable organizational
arrangement in any particular situation, and what was the best
method of achieving it, taking due account of a variety of personal
and local factors, were two different questions.

# Appendix B. The Social-Analytic Literature

The main published outcomes, up to the time of writing, from social-analytic work in the Glacier Project and the subsequent work centred on the Brunel Institute of Organization and Social Studies (BIOSS), are briefly identified below. Most are in book form, though a few papers are listed as well. No reference is made to a large accompanying stream of more ephemeral material. (For a fully comprehensive list of Glacier Project publications up to 1971, see Brown (1971), Bibliography; and for lists of the Brunel social-analytic and associated writing, see the various annual reports of the Brunel Institute of Organization and Social Studies.) The list is in chronological order of publication. Full bibliographical details of the publications listed are to be found in the References.

In compiling this list, the phrase 'social-analytic literature' has been interpreted in a broad sense. Publications have been included which deal with general theories or ideas underlying project-work, or with extrapolations of ideas derived from social-analytic project-work at some earlier stage, even though they do not refer to specific project-work itself. On the other hand, a number of detailed reports of systematic surveys of time-span or earning-progression material that have been undertaken outside a social-analytic framework are not included.[1]

*Changing Culture of a Factory* (Jaques, 1951) – a detailed report and analysis of the first three years of intensive project work at Glacier Metal. Discussion of elements at the institutional level intermingle

[1] For a review of this particular material, with detailed references, see Jaques (1976), *A General Theory of Bureaucracy*, pp. 164, 228–31.

freely with psychological interpretations. One of the early, often referred to, classics of the 'organization development' movement (*see* further description and comments in Chapter 1).

*Measurement of Responsibility* (Jaques, 1956) – a first report of how social-analytic work with members of Glacier Metal on grading, payment and progression problems led to the idea and definition of a new 'instrument' – 'time-span of discretion' – for measuring level of responsibility; to systematic data-gathering studies of the extant time-spans in various jobs; and to the beginnings of a statement of a general theory of the nature of work, responsibility in work, individual capacity, and payment.

*Exploration in Management* (Brown, 1960) – a major foundation stone for later social-analytic work. A systematic statement by the then Managing Director of Glacier Metal of the general organizational principles and concepts that had been developed within the Glacier Project and the organizational changes that had accompanied them. This book provides a principal reference for a general appreciation of the Glacier Project in its earlier formative years.

*Equitable Payment* (Jaques, 1961; 2nd edn., 1967) – subtitled 'a general theory of work, differential payment, and individual progression'. A further, more extensive and more general statement of the ideas broached in 'Measurement of Responsibility' and another of the principal theoretical foundations of all subsequent social-analytic work. Although all the ideas described grew in the first instance out of social-analytic discussions, they are supplemented with the findings of systematic surveys on 'felt-fair pay' levels, 'time-spans of discretion' and 'earning-progression curves'. (The second edition includes updated material on the actual techniques of time-span measurement.)

*Piecework Abandoned* (Brown, 1962) – a short but detailed review of one particular set of changes within the Glacier Project concerning payment systems, and the rationale for these changes.

*Product Analysis Pricing* (Brown and Jaques, 1964) – a report of another specific piece of work within the Glacier Project which moves from the analysis of the requisite organization necessary for the control of price fixing in a jobbing firm, to discussion in depth of specific methods of price fixing, i.e. in our terms from *institutional* to *programming* matters (*see* Chapter 3).

*Time-Span Handbook* (Jaques, 1964) – a short, practical guide to making time-span measurements as a basis for job grading.

*Glacier Project Papers* (Brown and Jaques, 1965) – a collection of articles and papers on certain broader ideas identified in the Glacier

Project, and their more widespread implications. Includes two pieces 'Speculations Concerning Level of Capacity' and 'Preliminary Sketch of a General Structure of Executive Strata' which have been particularly influential in stimulating subsequent theoretical development.

*Organization Analysis* (Newman and Rowbottom, 1968) – a first general text for students and other readers summarizing the main ideas in the Glacier Project, particularly as regards organizational structure, and deriving from experience of retailing these same ideas to various groups of visitors and students at the Glacier Institute of Management (*see* Chapter 1).

*Progression Handbook* (Jaques, 1968) – a short, practical guide to the technique of plotting individual earning-progressions, and its use in salary administration, staff selection, career-planning and man-power-planning.

*Work, Creativity and Social Justice* (Jaques, 1970) – a collection of essays on a mixture of psychological and social topics, with special emphasis on the nature of work, the psychological effects of work, disturbances of capacity to work, ideas of justice and equity within work, and the relevance of many psychoanalytic ideas to these topics.

*Organization* (Brown, 1971) – a major summation of the author's thinking and experience in this field, drawing heavily on Glacier Project material described in earlier publications, but also on other parts of the author's later experience, for example in national government. Its four main parts are entitled: 'The Anatomy of Employment Systems', 'Power Groups, Participation and Wage Differentials', 'Operational Work and Techniques' and 'Personnel Work and Techniques'.

*Working Relationships Within the British Hospital Service* (Kogan, Cang, Dixon and Tolliday, 1971) – a first and brief account of some of the varieties of organizational roles and relationships in hospitals discovered in an early Brunel-based research in this area, started in 1967.

*Working Papers on the Reorganization of the National Health Service* (Brunel Institute of Organization and Social Studies, Health Services Organization Research Unit, 1972) – a set of cyclostyled papers prepared mainly with the view in mind of offering analysis and elucidation of some of the specific organizational problems facing designers and implementors of the reorganized National Health Service which was introduced in 1974. Provides a general statement of project-thinking at that time as regards the main conceptions underlying the organization of health services. (Now out of print.)

*The Earnings Conflict* (Brown, 1973) – an extrapolation and generalization of some of the Glacier Project ideas into proposed models of the institutions, policies and procedures necessary for dealing with the problem of national regulation of wages. Includes also some important conceptual analyses of simple and complex associations, stable and unstable committees, and the general process of negotiation.

*Organization Design* (Newman, 1973) – a general text by the one-time Director of the Glacier Institute of Management based in part on Glacier Project ideas and in part on his own subsequent teaching and consultancy work.

*Hospital Organization* (Rowbottom, Balle, Cang, Dixon, Jaques, Packwood and Tolliday, 1973) – a more extended and comprehensive account of the first four years of the Brunel-based health research, with many details of specific field projects and of the conceptualization and models flowing from them.

*Social Services Departments – Developing Patterns of Work and Organization* (Brunel Institute of Organization and Social Studies, Social Services Organization Research Unit, 1974; principal authors: Rowbottom, Hey and Billis) – a comprehensive account of the first four years of the Brunel-based social services research, which started two years later than the health work, but ran thereafter in close interaction with it. (Thus, in a sense, this and 'Hospital Organization' form companion volumes.) Again, there are many details of specific project work and of conceptualizations and models arising from it.

*A General Theory of Bureaucracy* (Jaques, 1976) – a major summation of the author's thinking and experience in the field of human organizations. Deals with the massive phenomenon of bureaucratic organizations in modern society, its social and psychological bases, its contrast with the various kinds of association to which it is subservient, and its detailed structure and dynamics. The various ways in which bureaucracy may be made to forward the development and life of the individual at work, and the growth of social cohesion and trust, are considered in depth, and contrasted with the conventional view which sees bureaucracy as a generally undesirable and pathological manifestation. The whole thesis is related to a wide range of sociological, psychological, political and philosophical theory.

*Working Papers* (Brunel Institute of Organization and Social Studies, 1976–7) – a series of individually published cyclostyled papers

produced and distributed by the Health Services Organization
Research Unit and the Social Services Organization Research Unit.
Each paper presents a general synthesis of findings, ideas and models
based on a whole range of social-analytic field projects, together with
associated conference discussions. At the time of writing the published titles include:

(1) *Future Organization in Child Guidance and Allied Work*
(2) *Professionals in Health and Social Services Organization*
(3) *Collaboration Between Health and Social Services*
(4) *The Organization of Physiotherapy and Occupational Therapy in the
National Health Service*

Further papers are planned.

*The Stratification of Work and Organizational Design* (Rowbottom and
Billis, 1977) – a published paper describing a new general theory of
discrete work-strata in organizations, developed in the first instance
out of social services work at Brunel. Includes descriptions of some
applications of the concepts in specific project work in the same field.

*The Management of Human Capacity* (Evans, forthcoming) – commis-
sioned originally as a general review of the work and ideas of Elliott
Jaques, as part of a projected series on management thinkers, but
because of the failure of this project, to be published on its own.
Forms, in effect, a summary and appreciation in depth of the whole
of the 'work-pay-capacity' complex of ideas developed gradually in
previous work over the years.

# References

ARGYRIS, C. (1970), *Intervention Theory and Method, A Behavioural Science View*, Reading, Mass.: Addison-Wesley.

BANTON, M. (1965), *Roles, An Introduction to the Study of Social Relations*, London: Tavistock.

BECKER, H. S. (1970), *Sociological Work: Method and Substance*, London: Lane.

BECKHARD, R. (1969), *Organization Development, Strategies and Models*, Reading, Mass.: Addison-Wesley.

BENDIX, R. and LIPSET, S. M. (eds.) (1967), *Class, Status and Power*, 2nd edn., London: Routledge & Kegan Paul.

BENNIS, W. G. (1969), *Organization Development: Its Nature, Origins and Prospects*, Reading, Mass.: Addison-Wesley.

BENNIS, W. G., BENNE, K. D., and CHIN, R. (1970), *The Planning of Change*, 2nd edn., London: Holt, Rinehart and Winston.

BERGER, P. L. (1966), *Invitation to Sociology*, Harmondsworth: Penguin.

BERGER, P. L. and LUCKMAN, T. (1967), *The Social Construction of Reality*, London: Penguin.

BLAKE, R. R. and MOUTON, J. S. (1969), *Building a Dynamic Corporation Through Grid Organization Development*, Reading, Mass.: Addison-Wesley.

BLALOCK, H. M. (1970), *An Introduction to Social Research*, Englewood Cliffs, New Jersey: Prentice Hall.

BRADFORD, L. P., GIBB, J. R. and BENNE, K. D. (eds.) (1964), *T-Group Theory and Laboratory Method*, New York: Wiley.

BRAYBROOKE, D. and LINDBLOM, C. E. (1963), *A Strategy of Decision*, New York: Free Press.

BROWN, R. K. (1967), 'Research and Consultancy in Industrial Enterprises', *Sociology*, 1, 1, 33–60.

BROWN, W. (1960), *Exploration in Management*, London: Heinemann. (Reprinted as paperback, 1965, Harmondsworth: Penguin Books.)

BROWN, W. (1962), *Piecework Abandoned – The Effect of Wage Incentive Systems on Managerial Authority*, London: Heinemann.

BROWN, W. (1965), 'Informal Organizations?' in BROWN and JAQUES (1965).

BROWN, W. (1971), *Organization*, London: Heinemann.

BROWN, W. (1973), *The Earnings Conflict* – Proposals for Tackling the Emerging Crisis of Industrial Relations, Unemployment and Wage Inflation, London: Penguin.

BROWN, W. and JAQUES, E. (1964), *Product Analysis Pricing*, London: Heinemann.

BROWN, W. and JAQUES, E. (1965), *Glacier Project Papers*, London: Heinemann.

BROWN, W. and JAQUES, E. (1965a), 'Management Teaching' in BROWN and JAQUES (1965).

BRUNEL INSTITUTE OF ORGANIZATION AND SOCIAL STUDIES (1972), *Working Papers on The Reorganization of The National Health Service*, published by the Health Services Organization Research Unit.

BRUNEL INSTITUTE OF ORGANIZATION AND SOCIAL STUDIES, SOCIAL SERVICES ORGANIZATION RESEARCH UNIT (1974), *Social Services Departments: Developing Patterns of Work and Organization*, London: Heinemann.

BRUNEL INSTITUTE OF ORGANIZATION AND SOCIAL STUDIES (1976a), *Future Organization in Child Guidance and Allied Work, A Working Paper*, published jointly by the Health Services Organization Research Unit and the Social Services Organization Research Unit.

BRUNEL INSTITUTE OF ORGANIZATION AND SOCIAL STUDIES (1976b), *Professionals in Health and Social Services Organizations, A Working Paper*, published jointly by the Health Services Organization Research Unit and the Social Services Organization Research Unit.

BRUNEL INSTITUTE OF ORGANIZATION AND SOCIAL STUDIES (1976c), *Collaboration Between Health and Social Services, A Working Paper*, published jointly by the Health Services Organization Research Unit and the Social Services Organization Research Unit.

BRUNEL INSTITUTE OF ORGANIZATION AND SOCIAL STUDIES (1977), *The Organization of Physiotherapy and Occupational Therapy in the National Health Service, A Working Paper*, published by the Health Services Organization Research Unit.

BRUYN, S. T. (1966), *The Human Perspective in Sociology – The Methodology of Participant Observation*, Englewood Cliffs, N.J.: Prentice Hall.

BUBER, M. (1970), *I and Thou*, Translated with prologue and notes by Walter Kaufmann, Edinburgh: T. & T. Clark.

BURNS, T. and STALKER, G. M. (1961), *The Management of Innovation*, London: Tavistock Publications.

BURNS, T. (1970), 'Sociological Explanation' in EMMETT and MACINTYRE (1970).

CARO, F. G. (ed.) (1971), *Readings in Evaluation Research*, New York: Russell Sage.

CARR, E. H. (1964), *What Is History?*, London: Penguin.

CARTWRIGHT, D. and ZANDER, A. (eds.) (1968), *Group Dynamics: Research and Theory*, 3rd edn., London: Tavistock.

CHILD, J. (1972), 'Organizational Structure, Environment and Performance: The Role of Strategic Choice', *Sociology*, 6, 1, 2–22.

CICOUREL, A. V. (1964), *Method and Measurement in Sociology*, New York: Free Press.

CLARK, A. W. (1972), 'Sanction – A Critical Element in Action Research', *J. Applied Behavioural Science*, 8, 6, 713–29.

COCH, L. and FRENCH, J. R. P. (1948), 'Overcoming Resistance to Change' in CARTWRIGHT, D. and ZANDER, A. (1968).

DAHRENDORF, R. (1968), *Essays in the Theory of Society*, London: Routledge and Kegan Paul.

DAHRENDORF, R. (1968a), 'Homo Sociologicus' in *Essays in the Theory of Society*.

DAHRENDORF, R. (1968b), 'Values and Social Science' in *Essays in The Theory of Society*.

DAHRENDORF, R. (1968c), 'Out of Utopia, Towards a Re-orientation of Sociological Analysis', in *Essays in The Theory of Society*.

DAHRENDORF, R. (1968d), 'On the Origin of Inequality Among Men', in *Essays in The Theory of Society*.

DAHRENDORF, R. (1968e), 'Sociology and the Sociologist – On the Problem of Theory and Practice', in *Essays in the Theory of Society*.

DALE, A. T. (1974), 'Coercive Persuasion and the Role of the Change Agent', *Interpersonal Development*, 5, 102–11.

DALE, A. T. (1975), *What Is Organization Development?* Seminar Notes, Dale Loveluck Associates Ltd.

DEMERATH, N. J. and PETERSON, R. A. (eds.) (1967), *System, Change and Conflict*, New York: Free Press.

DENZIN, N. K. (1970), *The Research Act in Sociology*, London: Butterworth.

DEPARTMENT OF HEALTH AND SOCIAL SECURITY (1972), *Management Arrangements for the Re-organized Health Service*, London: HMSO.

DOUGLAS, J. D. (ed.) (1971), *Understanding Everyday Life – Towards the Reconstruction of Sociological Knowledge*, London: Routledge.

EASTON, D. (1971), *The Political System, An Inquiry into the State of Political Science*, 2nd edn., New York: *Alfred A. Knopf*.

EMERY, F. E. and THORSRUD, E. (1969), *Form and Content in Industrial Democracy*, London: Tavistock.

EMMETT, D. (1966), *Rules, Roles and Relations*, London: Macmillan.

EMMETT, D. and MACINTYRE, A. (eds.) (1970), *Sociological Theory and Philosophical Analysis*, London: Macmillan.

ETZIONI, A. (1964), *Modern Organizations*, Englewood Cliffs, N.J.: Prentice Hall.

EVANS, J. S. (1971), 'Contrasting Task Analysis Procedures in Consultancy-Based and Survey-Based Research', *Human Relations*, 24, 2, 139–48.

EVANS, J. S. (forthcoming), *The Management of Human Capacity*, MCB Publications.

FESTINGER, L. and KATZ, D. (1953), *Research Methods in the Behavioural Sciences*, New York: Holt, Rinehart.

FOSTER, P. M. (1972), 'An Introduction to the Theory and Practice of Action Research in Work Organizations', *Human Relations*, 25, 529–56.

FOX, A. (1974), *Beyond Contract: Work, Power and Trust Relationships*, London: Faber.

FRIEDMAN, N. (1967), *The Social Nature of Psychological Research*, New York: Basic Books.

GALTUNG, J. G. (1967), *Theory and Methods of Social Research*, New York, Columbia University Press.

GERTH, H. H. and MILLS, C. W. (1948), *From Max Weber*, London: Routledge and Kegan Paul.

GOODE, W. J. and HATT, P. K. (1953), *Methods in Social Research*, New York: McGraw Hill.

GROSS, N., MASON, W. S. and MCEACHERN, A. W. (1957), *Exploration in Role Analysis: Study of the School Superintendency Role*, New York: Wiley.

HAGE, J. and AIKEN, M. (1970), *Social Change in Complex Organizations*, New York: Random House.

HALMOS, P. (1965), *The Faith of the Counsellors*, London: Constable.

HERBST, P. G. (1974), *Socio-technical Design: Strategies in Multidisciplinary Research*, London: Tavistock.

HEY, A. and ROWBOTTOM, R. W. (1974), 'The Organization of Social Work in Hospitals and Other Health Care Settings', *Health and Social Services Journal*, 16 February 1974.

HORNSTEIN, H. A. *et al.* (eds.) (1971), *Social Intervention: A Behavioural Science Approach*, New York: The Free Press.

JAQUES, E. (ed.) (1947), 'Social Therapy' – A Special Issue of *Journal of Social Issues*, 3, 2.

JAQUES, E. (1951), *The Changing Culture of a Factory*, London: Tavistock Publications.

JAQUES, E. (1956), *Measurement of Responsibility*, London: Tavistock Publications.

JAQUES, E. (1964), *Time-Span Handbook*, London: Heinemann.

JAQUES, E. (1965a), 'Speculations Concerning Level of Capacity', in BROWN and JAQUES (1965).

JAQUES, E. (1965b), 'Preliminary Sketch of a General Structure of Executive Strata', in BROWN and JAQUES (1965).

JAQUES, E. (1965c), 'Social-Analysis and the Glacier Project', in BROWN and JAQUES (1965).

JAQUES, E. (1967), *Equitable Payment*, 2nd edn., Harmondsworth: Penguin.

JAQUES, E. (1968), *Progression Handbook* – How to Use Earnings Progression Data Sheets for Assessing Individual Capacity for Progression, and for Manpower Planning and Development, London: Heinemann.

JAQUES, E. (1970), *Work, Creativity and Social Justice*, London: Heinemann.

JAQUES, E. (1976), *A General Theory of Bureaucracy*, London: Heinemann.

KAHN, R. L., WOLFE, D. M., QUINN, R. P., SNOEK, J. D. and ROSENTHAL, R. A. (1964), *Organizational Stress: Studies in Role Conflict and Ambiguity*, New York: Wiley.

KOGAN, M., CANG, S., DIXON, M. and TOLLIDAY, H. (1971), *Working Relationships within the British Hospital Services*, London: Bookstall Publications.

LAKATOS, I. and MUSGRAVE, A. (eds.) (1970), *Criticism and the Growth of Knowledge*, London: Cambridge University Press.

LAWRENCE, P. R. and LORSCH, J. W. (1967), *Organization and Environment*, Boston: Harvard University Press.

LAWRENCE, P. R. and LORSCH, J. W. (1969), *Developing Organizations: Diagnosis and Action*, Reading, Mass.: Addison-Wesley.

LEAVITT, H. J. (1965), 'Applied Organizational Change in Industry: Structural, Technological and Humanistic Approaches', in MARCH, J. G. (ed.) (1965).

LIPPITT, R., WATSON, J. and WESTLEY, B. (1958), *The Dynamics of Planned Change*, New York: Harcourt Brace.

LITTERER, J. A. (ed.) (1969), *Organizations*, 2nd edn., New York: Wiley.

MACIVER, R. M. and PAGE, C. H. (1950), *Society: An Introductory Analysis*, London: Macmillan.

MANN, F. C. (1957), 'Studying and Creating Change', in Arensberg, C. M. *et al.* (eds.), *Research in Industrial Human Relations*, New York: Harper.

MARCH, J. G. (ed.) (1965), *Handbook of Organizations*, Chicago: Rand McNally.

MARRIS, P. and REIN, M. (1974), *Dilemmas of Social Reform*, 2nd edn., London: Penguin.

MERTON, R. K. (1968), *Social Theory and Social Structure*, 3rd edn., New York: Free Press.

MILES, M. B. *et al.* (1970), 'The Consequence of Survey Feedback: Theory and Evaluation', in BENNIS, BENNE and CHIN (1970).

MILLER, E. J. and RICE, A. K. (1967), *Systems of Organization*, London: Tavistock Publications.

MILLS, C. WRIGHT (1970), *The Sociological Imagination*, London: Penguin.

MITCHELL, G. D. (ed.) (1968), *A Dictionary of Sociology*, London: Routledge.

MORSE, N. C. and REIMER, E. (1956), 'The Experimental Change of a Major Organizational Variable', in LITTERER, J. A. (1969)

NEWMAN, A. D. and ROWBOTTOM, R. W. (1968), *Organization Analysis*, London: Heinemann.

NEWMAN, A. D. (1973), *Organizational Design*, London: Arnold.

NISBET, R. (1967), *The Sociological Tradition*, London: Heinemann.

PARSONS, T. (1951), *The Social System*, London: Routledge.

PEPPER, S. C. (1942), *World Hypotheses – A Study in Evidence*, Berkeley: University of California Press.

POPPER, K. R. (1961), *The Poverty of Historicism*, 2nd edn., London: Routledge & Kegan Paul.

POPPER, K. R. (1966), *The Open Society and Its Enemies*, 5th end., London: Routledge.

POPPER, K. R. (1974), *Conjectures and Refutations: The Growth of Scientific Knowledge*, 5th edn., London: Routledge.

PUGH, D. S., HICKSON, D. J. *et al.* (1963), 'A Conceptual Scheme for Organizational Analysis', *Admin. Sci. Q.*, 8, 4, 289–315.

PUGH, D. S. *et al.* (1968), 'Dimensions of Organization Structure', *Admin. Sci. Q.*, 13, 2, 65–105.

PUGH, D. S., HICKSON, D. J. and TURNER, C. (1969), 'The Context of Organization Structure', *Admin. Sci. Q.*, 14, 1, 91–114.

RAPOPORT, R. N. (1970), 'Three Dilemmas in Action Research – With Special Reference to the Tavistock Experience', *Human Relations*, 23, 6, 499–513.

REVANS, R. W. (1976), *Action Learning in Hospitals: Diagnosis and Therapy*, London: McGraw Hill.

RICE, A. K. (1963), *The Enterprise and Its Environment*, London: Tavistock Publications.

ROSENTHAL, R. (1966), *Experimenter Effects in Behavioural Research*, New York: Appleton-Century Crofts.

ROWBOTTOM, R. W. *et al.* (1973), *Hospital Organization*, A Progress Report on the Brunel Project, London: Heinemann.

ROWBOTTOM, R. W. and BILLIS, D. (1977), 'The Stratification of Work and Organizational Design', *Human Relations*, 30, 1, 53–76.

RUNCIMAN, W. G. (1971), *Social Science and Political Theory*, 2nd edn., London: Cambridge University Press.

RYAN, ALAN (1970), *The Philosophy of the Social Sciences*, London: Macmillan.

RYCROFT, C. (ed.) (1968), *Psychoanalysis Observed*, London: Penguin.

SCHEIN, E. H. (1969), *Process Consultation: Its Role in Organization Development*, Reading, Mass.: Addison-Wesley.

SCHUTZ, A. (1972), *The Phenomenology of the Social World*, London: Heinemann.

SELLTIZ, C. *et al.* (1965), *Research Methods in Social Relations*, Revised edn., London: Methuen.

SILVERMAN, D. (1970), *The Theory of Organization*, London: Heinemann.

SIMEY, T. S. (1968), *Social Science and Social Purpose*, London: Constable.

STACEY, M. (1969), *Methods of Social Research*, Oxford: Pergamon Press.

SUCHMAN, E. A. (1967), *Evaluation Research: Principles and Practice in Public Service and Social Action Programs*, New York: Russell Sage.

SUMNER, W. (1959), *Folkways*, New York: Dover.

SZASZ, T. (1974), *Ideology and Insanity*, London: Penguin.

TOULMIN, S. (1953), *The Philosophy of Science*, London: Hutchinson.

TRIST, E. L. (1967), 'Engaging With Large-Scale Systems: Some Concepts and Methods Based on Experience Gained in Field Projects at the Tavistock Institute.' A Paper. London: Tavistock Institute of Human Relations.

TURNER, R. (ed.) (1974), *Ethnomethodology*, London: Penguin.

WEBER, M. (1964), *The Theory of Social and Economic Organization*, New York: The Free Press.

WESTLEY, W. A. (1975), 'An Analytic-Inductive Model for Evaluation Research', McGill University, Montreal.

WESTLEY, W. A. (1975), 'Dialogue with Reality: A Study of Social Analysis', McGill University, Montreal.

WINCH, P. (1958), *The Idea of A Social Science*, London: Routledge.

WOODWARD, J. (1965), *Industrial Organization: Theory and Practice*, London: Oxford University Press.

# Index